Right from the start

A service for families with a young handicapped child

Editors: **Bernie Spain**
Guy Wigley

Technical Editor: Victoria Shennan

The National Society for Mentally Handicapped Children acknowledges the generous support of The King's Fund and The Spastics Society in the production of this Report.

ISBN 0 855 37027 0

Copies of this publication are obtainable from
The NSMHC Bookshop, 17 Pembridge Square, London W2 4EP
Price: £1.25

Printed by Green & Co (Lowestoft) Ltd, Crown St., Lowestoft.

contents

Foreword

As the re-organised National Health Service struggles with mounting costs and the needs of families under stress become ever more acute, all the available resources of the community must be marshalled to give the maximum possible return.

Bernie Spain and Guy Wigley have collected data and made recommendations which are valuable and timely, and have performed a real service for those who must plan for the future.

We are sure that all parents with a child suffering from handicap will benefit if the advice given is heeded.

This Society has for long been concerned with "early intervention" and has been insistent on the importance of a comprehensive programme for the very young mentally handicapped child. It was because of this that we were happy to publish Gunnar Dybwad's views on the subject ("The Mentally Handicapped Child under Five"), and it is for the same reason that we are glad that this work also is to appear under the Society's imprint.

GEORGE W. LEE OBE
Secretary General
National Society for Mentally
Handicapped Children

Introduction

The purpose of this publication is practical; it is to help mobilise better support for the families of children who are found to be severely handicapped from any cause at birth or soon after. This is no small problem—in the average health district of 200,000 there will probably be about 50 children each year born with a congenital malformation recognisable at birth and a further 32 a year having an abnormality detectable in the the first seven years of life.

It has been truly remarked that the birth of a handicapped child creates a handicapped family. But many, and perhaps even most, of these families are more distressed than need be the case because we have failed to provide the help, at once sensitive and practical, which they so acutely needed right from the start. And so in grief, anger and despair attitudes are formed towards the child, harmful both to his potential development and to the quality of family life. In countries with complex advanced medical and social services responsibility for care is shared between a number of professional people, rarely organised in a true multi-disciplinary team. Consequently, in these countries, the lonely reality of caring for a handicapped child at home, and the necessity for personal involvement with the parents' shock and grief is least likely to be appreciated, and so help is not given when it is needed most.

Parents commonly report that it is in the first few months and years after the diagnosis has been made, while they are still trying to comprehend its implications, that they experience the most urgent need for support and explanation, but that it is precisely during the child's early years when the support services are weakest. In fact, while parents praise the more technical aspects of the health service, they feel that throughout the child's life there is a continual lack of discussion of the child's condition and of practical advice on the management of the child at home. This book aims to define the situation which parents face, to suggest ways in which they may be met and above all to set out a clear administrative framework within which the service can be provided. A proper administrative structure is essential since a major problem at present is the failure to designate clearly just who is responsible for communicating with families the salient facts about a child's prognosis or the services available.

INTRODUCTION

Within the reorganised health service it should be easier to provide this type of advice and continuity than was possible previously with a split between the three arms of the service and with so little contact between hospital and extra-hospital personnel. We feel that while many improvements in the children's services have taken place in recent years little has been done to ameliorate this aspect of the problem and decided that at this point it would be useful to review the whole issue, in order to make some constructive suggestions about how the help to such families might be improved following the reorganisation of the health service. A number of distinguished people from differing professions and known to have an interest in this field were invited to come together for discussion and later to write short papers which between them cover the background. These form part one of the publication and, so they say, set the scene.

At a later date, after the contributors had had an opportunity to read each other's papers, which were pre-circulated, they met, together with a number of colleagues, to hold a recorded discussion which was also attended by observers from the main voluntary bodies concerned and from the Department of Health.

Part two is our synopsis of what took place at that meeting. Inevitably, spontaneous verbal discussion leaves many a hiatus and points which appear to be made with crystal clarity at the time read oddly in the recorded script and for those reasons a synoptic approach was preferred to an attributable verbatim record. Our script was sent to selected people for comment, some of them administrators, others clinicians, and we are deeply grateful for all the very considerable and painstaking help we got from them which has filled out and polished our final text. Inevitably, this has led to a certain bland flatness of style and, because we were striving for consensus and comprehensive cover, to a presentation perhaps a little reminiscent of a central government circular.

The Recommendation section is written specifically for implementation within the context of the National Health Service. It would need to be adapted to fit other administrative structures but the advantages of suggesting a clear cut administrative process applicable universally within the National Health Service overrode all other considerations and, indeed, this had been our goal from the beginning for we see it as the key to action.

One Appendix contains accounts written by parents of handicapped children of their experiences with the medical services. It would be difficult indeed to be complacent about the problem after reading them. We are grateful to *The Lancet* for allowing us to use one of these, and to Mervyn Fox for supplying the others.

We are aware that in some parts of the country an attempt has already been made to introduce some changes on the lines we are suggesting and Appendix 3 gives details of such schemes developed for spina bifida children, who, with their multiple deformities, exemplify the problems involved in caring for the handicapped child. The contributions on the specialist health visitors will give nurse administrators much to ponder over.

The use of behaviour modification techniques in child management has created much interest in recent years and Appendix IV gives an account of its use at Hilda Lewis House in relation to the care of mentally handicapped children in their own homes.

The present acute shortage of money for the health and social services is frustrating for those involved and wishing for many improvements. We hope that this publication will give guidance to those seeking to make a significant improvement to the quality of the service without great additional expenditure. For this reason we hope that this book will be read by Community Health Council members no less than by members of Area Health Authorities, paediatricians, community physicians and nursing officers, as well as staff from Social Services Departments who would, of course, be vitally concerned with implementation of these recommendations.

BERNIE SPAIN
GUY WIGLEY

Paper One

THE FEELINGS AND BEHAVIOUR OF PARENTS OF HANDICAPPED CHILDREN

Ronald MacKeith
Paediatrician

The behaviour of parents of handicapped children derives from many factors. These include cultural and social-class attitudes to children in general, to handicapped people and to teachers, social workers and to doctors and medical care in general. But to a major degree, their behaviour derives from their feelings about having a handicapped child.

Whatever the handicap, the reactions of parents to all the varieties of handicapped children have much that is similar.

The reactions will be influenced by whether the handicap is evident at birth or becomes evident later, after the parents have 'fallen in love' with the child. They will be influenced by whether there is a prospect of severe mental handicap or not. They will be influenced by whether the handicap is obvious to other people, and by the attitudes of other people – including lay people, teachers, social workers and doctors – to handicap and to handicapped people.

Parents' feelings

What may be the reaction of parents who find their child is handicapped? What will the feelings (and hence the behaviour) of a couple who find themselves in what may be called a 'classical' or typical situation. Consider the reactions of a young couple who have as their first child one with Down's syndrome or spina bifida – handicaps which are evident at birth. They have not yet 'fallen in love' in a way that means the child is part of them whatever happens to him. Their feelings will be mixed ones.

1 *Biological reactions:* protection of the helpless; revulsion at the abnormal.
2 *Feelings of inadequacy:* inadequacy at reproduction; inadequacy at rearing.
3 *Feelings of bereavement:* at the loss of the normal child they expected,

with almost infinite potentialities: (a) anger; (b) grief; and (c) adjustment, which takes time.

4 *Feeling of shock.*
5 *Feeling of guilt:* which is probably less common than many writers state.
6 *Feeling of embarrassment:* which is a social reaction to what the parents think other people are feeling.

Parents' behaviour

1 (*a*) The biological reaction of protectiveness towards the helpless infant will tend to produce 'maternal' behaviour in both the mother and the father: (i) frequently there is *warm normal care*: or (ii) there may be *highly protective care.* Labelling highly protective care as over-protection is not an observation but a judgement and should involve the mother's need to behave in this way and the child's need to be highly protected.
(*b*) The biological reaction of revulsion at the abnormal is a normal reaction, even if in our culture it is frowned upon. It will produce rejection of the child. Rejection may show itself as: (i) *cold rejection*; (ii) *rationalised rejection*, the parents suggesting that the child should be 'in a home with specially trained people to care for him'; (iii) *dutiful caring* without warmth; or (iv) *lavish care* from over-compensation of the feeling of rejection.

2 (*a*) Feelings of inadequacy at reproduction can strike deep at a person's self-respect and may produce *depression.*
(*b*) Feelings of inadequacy at rearing can produce *lack of confidence and hence inconsistency of rearing.*

3 (*a*) The anger of bereavement may cause *aggressive behaviour* towards those who are trying to help the parents.
(*b*) The grief may cause *depression.*
(*c*) The *adjustment* may come fairly quickly and though often stable is not always so in face of problems that arise later.

4 The sense of shock may cause *disbelief* and *a succession of consultations at other clinics in the search for better news.*

5 Guilt is frequently written about but it is not felt by all parents. It is a complex feeling with undertones, for example of punishment. It can produce *depression.*

6 Embarrassment can lead to *withdrawal from social contacts* and consequent social isolation.

Feelings and behaviour of professional advisers

Nurses, social workers, teachers, therapists and doctors faced with a handicapped person are often disturbed, as are most adults. As with parents, their behaviour will be influenced by their feelings. Social workers and doctors can feel revulsion at the abnormal and, having these feelings, show them in *recommending the parents to put the child away into a home* when this is not what the parents would choose. The family's advisers may be over-solicitous about the child and *forget the needs of the rest of the family.*

Doctors may reveal their own feelings of inadequacy at caring for the child by *brusque dismissal of the child and parents.* Doctors may also reveal their sense of inadequacy by objecting to the parents 'shopping around' for a further opinion. A doctor who feels he is reasonably competent and who has given adequate attention and time to the parents may regret that he has failed to meet their needs, but he will understand why they feel they must ask for a further opinion. He may wonder where he failed them, but he will convey his understanding of their desire and will help them to see another physician. He will also convey very clearly that he is willing to accept them back again at any time.

Should the child go away from home?

Sometimes parents ask for this when they first know – at the birth of the child – that he is lastingly handicapped. It seems best to convey that there is no urgency to make a permanent decision. They may leave the child in hospital and later take him home, or they may take him home earlier with the knowledge that the physican will re-admit the child to hospital at any time.

Later on, the decision will depend on three principles which are presented to the parents.

(*a*) In our culture, most people live with their families and do better if they do so.
(*b*) People go away from home if thereby they are able to get treatment and education which are better – and sufficiently better to outweigh the disadvantages of being away from home.
(*c*) People go away from home if other people in the family are suffering from their continued presence.

These general principles can be conveyed over the years, long before any decision is urgently needed.

Crisis periods during growth

Crisis periods are important to know about, for the professional adviser can himself be prepared to act to diminish the difficulties of parents at these times. Furthermore, at the times of crisis, parents are often more open to receiving helpful guidance.

1 *When parents first learn about or suspect handicap* in their child. Until their anxieties are (to some extent) dealt with by full assessment and explanation, their child is 'not a person but a question mark'. This is a doctor's job.
2 When, *at about age five*, a decision has to be reached as to whether the child will be able to go to ordinary school, which would be a 'certificate' that he is more or less normal. This decision is reached by psychologists, educationalists and doctors in collaboration.
3 When the handicapped person comes to *the time of leaving school*: both the parents and the handicapped person realise that cure is never going to happen and they wonder whether he or she will be independent and able to work, while the handicapped person wonders whether he or she will be able to meet girls or boys, make love and marry. Some of the explanation will fall on the employment services, some on social workers and some on doctors.
4 *When the parents become older* and are unable to care for their handicapped child. Parents will look ahead anxiously and they deserve to be reminded that there are statutory services which will give help.

Support for the parents

Support for the parents is one of the major needs that therapists, teachers, social workers and doctors have to provide. Perhaps the support given in the earliest days and months is of crucial importance for long-term acceptance by the parents. Their questions must be answered but they will also be greatly helped if they are shown how they themselves can be helping their child every day to move towards achieving his full potential.

For the community, there are economic benefits to be gained from giving full support and help to the parents but, more important, this is a compassionate and necessary part of the care of the handicapped person and his family.

Paper Two

STATING THE PROBLEM

Robert Wigglesworth,
Paediatrician

What are the basic facts of the situation? Many of us speak and have spoken of the mother-child relationship as though it started with the birth of the child. There may be those mothers of imagination and sensitivity, who feel a relationship with another individual they have helped to create, from the moment of the intercourse which leads to conception. This I feel must be a minority, although I have little personal knowledge on which to base this statement and I do not know of any research into this. In fact, research into what might be described as the consumer side of the process of bringing the next human generation into being, is singularly deficient, perhaps in indirect proportions to its importance: as is perhaps so true of so much of our approach to the basic problems of life on our planet Earth.

In my experience of discussing pregnancy with mothers, I believe that for most, the relationship begins at the fifth month or twentieth week, with the moment of quickening, when the mother first feels in a direct and tangible way, the movements of the living child within her. Mothers have told me that from this moment, they never again feel alone day or night until the infant is born, when the child is again revealed to the mother through the other senses of sight and sound. The responsibility of socially caring for another helpless human being, of the mother's own partial creation, also begins at this moment of birth.

Although the mother may have been aware of the importance of her contribution to the health and well being of her child before the moment of birth, this has been at an automatic, parasite host level. This is in contrast to the full social giving of herself in her feeding and nurturing care after birth, and her vital role in teaching her infant all the basic learning for life. The early relationship of the mother following the quickening is at the emotionally highly significant sensory level of touch and movement, which as in all human interrelationships are far more significant and moving (no accident the use of that word) than vision, hearing and smell, and then are phylo-genetically earlier and more basic.

The importance of these observations lies in the fact that when we tell the mother anything about her baby, whether it is average or exceptional in some way, we are not speaking about a stranger, but about an individual human life the mother has known well, at a deep emotional level and who has indeed been a part of herself and her body image in an odd separate sort of way for at least four months if not longer. I think this may be of particular significance in the way we handle the birth of a stillborn infant. It is no use pretending to ourselves the infant has never existed and the whole episode is best forgotten, and the least said the sooner mended. This at least will not fool the mother concerned. She probably needs to be allowed the full human dignity of being given, if not positively encouraged to have an opportunity of grieving for her lost infant.

It is also important in the way we discuss with the mother her newborn baby. Just occasionally, an understanding mother may have sensed that something is wrong with her unborn infant, because for example of the paucity of the movements or of some feeling she cannot explain verbally. As far as I can gather, many, if not most, mothers have had fantasies of their unborn infant being abnormal, not right, or perhaps the more dramatic Celts will say 'of being a monster'. Hence the question many mothers ask, especially if given an appropriate, uninhibited opportunity of talking to the midwife or paediatrician – '*Is he or she all right.*' We therefore arrive at the point where we realise the importance of telling the mother about her baby after birth, even when everything has gone well, and we have a beautiful normal baby to present to the mother for her careful visual inspection, not forgetting the importance of allowing and encouraging body contact in holding the baby close, feeling and observing the body movements, hearing all the sounds and smelling the smells. Hence also the importance of rooming-in, for mother and baby to get to know each other well, and especially so in hospital births with an early discharge scheme, before they are projected back into their homes, perhaps after an abrupt and artificial separation following birth.

Involving the father

Telling about the birth of an abnormal child is infinitely more difficult and demanding, but needs to be done against a background of normal physiology and psychology. You will have noticed that I have concentrated so far on telling the *mother*, who is most immediately available and most intimately and immediately concerned. Nevertheless, it is my practice whenever this is possible, (and I cannot emphasise enough that this is a performance which simply has to be played by ear, sensing all the shifting emotions which are being involved and acted out), to tell the *father* about an obviously congenitally abnormal baby first. I then ask him whether he would like to break the news to his wife with me present, or on his own, or would he prefer me to do it in his presence or alone.

The father is more detached and less intimately involved emotionally with the child at this crisis stage, but nevertheless, when first told the news, it is the fathers who faint and not the mothers; so much so that I have learned always to see that the father is seated in a secure chair, with sides, before I impart the news. As a medical student at Barts however, I soon learned that it was the hefty Smithfield meat market porters, who fainted when I stitched up their cuts, not the thin, pale looking, fragile teenage girls who worked in the City sewing and machinery workshops. The children of the family also need to be told about their new baby sibling, but the parents can often be later instructed how to do this themselves. Nevertheless, casual opportunities of meeting the siblings should not be lost and the opportunity taken of testing the situation and helping them in their attitude towards their handicapped sibling.

This, of course, implies ongoing counselling and care of all handicapped families (i.e. a family with a handicapped member – baby – sibling or other member) and this I believe is a necessity. It is essential in those families where the crisis situation presents, with the birth of an obvious congenitally abnormal child, as well as in those where the diagnosis is in doubt or cannot be made for certainty until later in infancy or childhood. It is just as essential when a handicap is acquired later in infancy or childhood.

Breaking the news

Who is to do the telling? Who is to do the ongoing counselling, which I think should be combined with total care? The obstetrician is often not present at the birth of an abnormal child, and if he is the mother is often anaesthetised and unconscious. Anyway he often feels he has delivered a faulty end-product after subconsciously expecting to present to the mother a source of great joy. The midwife is most often the person present at an infant's birth, be it normal or abnormal. Very often she can be the best person to break the news to the mother, but if she does, she will need to be instructed in the art and science of doing so, and she herself will often need support and help in this demanding task. Above all, she must beware of non-verbal communication to the mother, as with the midwife who said nothing but showed her horror at the sight of a spina bifida baby, in her eyes above her mask and by hustling the baby away into a cot, as one mother told me.

Some paediatricians can be the best choice for this irksome and exhausting task of telling the family, particularly when they are going to be involved in the subsequent care, follow up, assessment, treatment, counselling and total management. They are unlikely to be present at the birth, although almost always in properly organised departments of paediatrics and child health, a junior member of the paediatric staff is present at abnormal and high risk category births.

Some delay in the mother being told can be advantageous, in allowing her to recover from the anaesthesia, the exhaustion of the delivery and the emotional impact of the birth. This makes it easier to mobilise the presence of a consultant paediatrician, or family doctor, according to who is considered the most appropriate person in the whole circumstances of the individual situation.

It is fortunate when the telling of the family can be done after the legally recognised period of maternal emotional instability following the birth of a child (i.e. six weeks) is over. Obviously this is frequently impossible and perhaps some would say, on doubtful psychological grounds, that it is unnecessary to worry about this period. Quite clearly in any retrospective enquiry directed to find out when the mother or family would have preferred to be told about a handicapped child, the answer will nearly always be 'as early as possible.' In such an enquiry the dynamics of the current and perhaps critical situation, are either well forgotten or safely dealt with by subsequent protective and healing psychological processes of the mind.

Paper Three

THE BIRTH OF AN ABNORMAL CHILD

Margaret Pollak
General Practitioner

Is it possible to define an ideal system of care for the handicapped child and his family? It might be seen as a continuous – and continuing – process whereby the full medical knowledge and therapeutic requirements of the condition, at the varying stages of the disease and the child's development, are readily and sympathetically available. There would be a constant supervision of the family to ensure that they have full knowledge of – and access to – the social amenities which are available for their help; but, above all, there would be provision of informed and compassionate advice and counsel so that the parents having recovered from their initial shock and grief, can sustain and enjoy their role of parenthood to the handicapped child and the child can come to maturity enriched by a childhood during which everything possible has been done to enable him to realise his full potential, so that he is not only a person in his own right but an accepted member of society. It is important that his siblings will not have suffered by his presence but will have benefited from a positive relationship with him; and, lastly, society will have learned that the handicapped have something to give as well as to take and that tolerance without pity is required.

It will readily be admitted that these aims, at the present time, are largely unmet. There are many reasons why this is so, and, perhaps by analysing some of the inadequate future remedies will be suggested.

Breaking the news

The majority of babies are born in hospitals, so that, in the case of physical deformities immediately apparent at birth, the responsibility for breaking the news will belong to the hospital. In the past, this unpleasant task has too often been left to the young, unskilled houseman. Moreover, the time for telling has often been left until just prior to discharge. Since the majority of parents are unable to accept the full implications of the facts at the first interview, this timing is unsatisfactory, as it does not allow for more than one interview.

There has been a less than satisfactory communication between the hospital doctor on the one hand and the general practitioner and local authority doctor on the other. It seems important that the two latter should be alerted not only to the diagnosis, but also to what the parents have been told, and how they reacted to the news.

There will, however, be a proportion of children in whom the functional handicap will only reveal itself by a delay in appearance. It is for the early detection of these children that developmental screening clinics have their raison d'etre. It seems, to the present writer, irrelevant who does these screening processes, so long as they *are* done. In the past, general practitioners who have such clinics have been few and far between and the brunt of the work has been carried out by local authority departments. An excellent start has been made, but so often, follow-up has been a voluntary act on the part of the parents, and much of what should be a medical examination has been left to health visitors.

Early days at home

For the family doctor, this is the most important time of all. The parents need immediate psychological support and at this time will begin the basis of the doctor-patient relationship. Thus, correct management is vital. The importance of a good working relationship between the family and their family doctor and health visitor cannot be over-emphasised, since these two workers will bear the main brunt of the future care. There must be a prevention of 'shopping around' by the parents for a more hopeful diagnosis. Although the role of the family doctor and health visitor, at this stage, appears paramount, it has not always been so. There has been a serious lack of realization of the needs, but this is not altogether surprising in view of the sparse training of both medical students and health visitors in the care of the handicapped child.

In the longer term

The grief reaction over, there is now a need for practical advice, both in the medical and social sphere, so that teamwork will be required. Health visitors, social workers, the special societies, family doctors, paediatricians and community physicians will all provide differing help at varying times, and this will require both staying power and enthusiasm, but, above all, one single person whose special task it is to draw all these varying disciplines and ideas together. There are many reasons why, in the past, the stage has been incorrectly managed. Parents have been unaware of amenities available and how to get them, although teamwork is the cry of the day, so often it has been lip service only.

There is a feeling of hopelessness and inadequacy on the part of the medical profession, probably due to lack of knowledge and experience; hospital follow-up has been relegated to each succeeding new houseman. The family doctor has concerned himself only with the crisis situations of the child, and local authority doctors have been greatly hampered by the scarcity of places in special schools or nursery places. Ordinary schools have felt unable to accept the challenge of handicapped children in their midst and there has been difficulty in staffing long-term care homes.

Adolescence

Mention must be made of this stage, since it is, so often, the most difficult of all the stages. The handicapped child is no longer the appealing baby, but a growing teenager, apparently the concern of no-one. At the same time, he is becoming acutely aware of himself vis-a-vis his peers, so that depression and behaviour problems are frequent at this stage. The present provision of sheltered workshops and leisure activities for the handicapped is almost non-existent.

Guidelines

It becomes apparent, thus, that there *are* some broad guidelines for the improvement in the future. First and foremost, there is a need for more learning and experience. The curriculum of the medical undergraduate must be altered to encompass the care of the handicapped, much more than has been in the past. The same point applies to the teaching of health visitors and social workers.

It has probably, in the past, not been fully realised by all the varying disciplines, that the need for care is multi-factorial, and needs to be thought of in medical, psychological and social terms. Perhaps, because of this generic nature, the core of the problem lies here, since it thus requires the continuing availability of re-assessment and encouragement in all these spheres. Such a service requires the co-operation and skills of varying disciplines and this brings with it the need to know and respect others in the team. The present writer deplores the glib bandying about of words such as 'team approach', 'multi-disciplinary care' as though the mere pronunciation produces the effect. It has to be seen that such co-operation requires a high degree of skill and goodwill from all members of the team if the patient is to receive maximum help.

POLLACK

There is an apparent need for a structure in the care of the handicapped so that it is the task of some one person to see that deficiencies and neglect do not occur.

There is also a need for society to be educated to accept the handicapped in their midst.

Paper Four

TELLING THE FAMILY
a review of some relevant research and opinion

Sheila Hewett
Psychologist

The moment when parents have to learn that their child is suffering from a permanently handicapping condition is a moment of crisis. The problem is to meet this crisis more helpfully than is at present the case. The moment to tell the diagnosis may come at different stages in the child's life and it is useful to classify these in terms of the condition of the child. (Carr and Oppe, 1971):

Group One
Conditions obvious to all at birth – parents as well as professionals. These would include almost all spina bifidas, some hydrocephalies, skeletal deformities, absence of limbs, absence or deformities of external organs, mid-line deformities, Apert's Syndrome and others.

Group Two
Conditions not so obvious at birth, particularly to parents and sometimes to doctors. These include Down's Syndrome, other chromosomal anomalies, some cerebral palsies, microcephaly, dislocations and so on.

Group Three
The 'emergent' handicapping conditions. *These are by far the largest group* and include mental retardation, most cerebral palsies, hearing disabilities, impairments of vision, epilepsy, metabolic disorders, some heart conditions – all present at birth but diagnosed at varying intervals after the perinatal period – many of them as long as one to two years later.

Children in Group One force a duty on doctors, hospital staff and midwives immediately to explain the condition and to explain surgical implications if necessary. How well is this done? Evidence comes from parents and from professionals, either from research findings or from observation in clinical settings.

Hare et al. (1966) first contacted 120 mothers of spina bifida children within three days of the birth. At a one-month follow-up interview, 80% of mothers felt they had been told kindly, but only 50% thought they had been told enough. Ninety per cent thought it right to be told straight away, although initially they had been able to take in very little beyond the fact that a handicapping condition was present. This emphasizes the importance of following up the initial telling. Hare et al., place the responsibility for deciding when and how much to tell firmly on the medical and nursing staff but comments that lack of training for this task and in some cases the anxieties and emotions of staff themselves can lead to clumsy, hurtful and ineffectual encounters with parents (vide Thurston, 1959, 1960 Quilliam, 1964). Meadow and Hewitt (1972) report on new approaches to teaching communication skills to medical students.

Freeston (1971) reports from Sheffield that out of 47 mothers of children with spina bifida, 25 said they had been told first by nurses and 11 by doctors. Quilliam (1964) and Davis (1964) in a related context, suggest that doctors leave explanation to nursing staff because they find discussions with parents boring and time consuming, unlike interesting technico-medical aspects of the condition. Peter Tizard (1968) claims that if doctors 'on occasion' fail to give adequate information, it is because they do not have enough time and that the 'bad press' doctors receive is not justified. He suggests that psychologists are not fit persons to discuss the matter, which should be left to psychiatrists.

One psychiatrist (Goldie, 1966), reporting on three handicapped children referred to him, emphasized the needs of the parents for practical and emotional help and for better information. Doctors who had seen the children previously had not understood these needs, nor the need for support after a child had left home for long-term care. (Hewett, 1972).

Children in the Groups Two and Three have conditions which mean that parents have had, in many cases, a period of anxiety and uncertainty before the diagnosis was made. Carr (1970) presents clear evidence that most of these mothers wish to know as soon as possible that something is wrong with the child. She summarises evidence from Franklin (1963), Evans (1962), Fortune (1962), Jacobs (1962), Hare (1966), Drillien and Wilkinson (1964), and Cowie (1966), to corroborate her own findings. Barsch (1968), Hewett (1970, 1972) and McMichael (1971) provide supporting evidence. Carr shows that parents' satisfaction with how they were told correlates well with being told early in the child's life.

In spite of the evidence, some doctors believe that mothers should not be told so soon. (Gunther in Prechtl 1963, Gath 1968.)

A majority of mothers in all surveys feel that not enough time and thought is given either to the initial telling or to the discussion of what it means. Advice and information must be comprehensible. MacKeith (1967) advocates giving parents 'time and an accepting, relaxed and comfortable atmosphere' in a Developmental Paediatrics Centre.

Continued counselling

Whenever one decides to tell, great care must be exercised over what is said (Kershaw 1966, Nash 1968). Hewett (1972) found a relationship between prognoses seen as 'hopeless' by the parents and subsequent institutionalisation of the child, although it is not suggested that the relationship is a simple causal one. Nash (1968) warns against 'careless comment' when babies with spina bifida are born, saying it may 'queer the pitch for reasoned discussion' later.

Some mothers (Hewett 1970) and some doctors (Kershaw 1966) believe the GP is the person to follow up the consultants' efforts to communicate with the parents. This follow-up is perhaps more important than the initial telling and it is axiomatic that it must be accompanied by practical help and advice. Counselling without comprehensible information and practical help is of little value. (Henderson 1968, Matheny and Vernick 1969, Bobath and Finnie 1970.)

Health visitors claim that they can do all that social workers can, except 'case work' and that social workers (except medical social workers) are unwilling even to acknowledge the existence of health visitors (Clark 1973). Mothers, however, tend not to see health visitors as very helpful (Hewett 1970, Wing 1973, Brugh 1971, Walker et al. 1971, Carr 1970). Jackson et al. (1973) and Carr and Oppe (1971) suggest that many people must be prepared and sufficiently well informed to answer questions, since parents are too diffident to approach consultants.

All surveys, from that of the Carnegie United Kingdom Trust (1964) to Brugh (1971) emphasise the gaps in services to handicapped children and their families. Orwell (1973) contacted 42 Directors of Social Service Departments and found that there are still wide differences between local authorities in their efforts to implement the Chronically Sick and Disabled Persons Act (1971). Martin and Rehin (1969) showed that the counselling service that was necessary still did not exist. Younghusband et al. (1970) also emphasise gaps in services and suggest remedies. There is evidence of complacency in some areas (NAMH report 1964), one LA mental health worker claiming that provision for mentally handicapped children far from being inadequate was 'almost generous'. He was replying to an agonised personal account of problems met by parents but not helped by the social services.

The evidence that problems continue to exist both for parents and professionals is overwhelming and cannot be ignored. Heavy case loads for doctors, health visitors and social workers argue that there should be a special team in each local authority area, (possibly of health visitors and social workers) trained to advise and inform parents, trained to get and to pass on information to them, and trained to over-ride boundaries between one service and another. It could be the duty of the Health Authorities and the Social Service Departments jointly to see that this is done. The inclusion of some parents on such a team might increase its usefulness.

References

BARSCH, R. H., 1968. 'The Parent of the Handicapped Child'. Charles C. Thomas Springfield, U.S.A.

BOBATH, B. and FINNIE, N. R., 1970. 'Problems of communication between parents and staff in the treatment of management of children with cerebral palsy'. *Devel. Med. Child Neurol.* **12**, 5, 629–35.

BURGH, A., 1971. 'Handicapped Children and their Families'. A report on medical and community services for handicapped children in a London Borough and attending the assessment clinic of a London teaching hospital. Unpublished.

CARNEGIE UNITED KINGDOM TRUST REPORT 1964. 'Handicapped children and their Families' 14. Dunfermline.

CARR, J., 1970. 'Mongolism – Telling the Parents'. *Devel. Med. Child Neurol.* **12**, 213–221.

CARR and OPPE, 1971. 'The Birth of an Abnormal Child – Telling the Parents'. Report of a N.A.M.H. Working Party. *Lancet*, November 13th, 1971.

CLARK, J., 1973. 'A Family Visitor'. Royal College of Nursing – London. Reviewed in *New Society*, 5th April, 1973.

COWIE, V., 1966. 'Genetic Counselling'. *Proc. Roy. Soc. Med.* **59**, 149.

DAVIS, J. A., 1964. 'The Attitude of Parents to the Approaching Death of their Child. *Devel. Med. Child. Neurol.* **6**, 286.

DRILLIEN, C. M. and WILKINSON, E. M., 1964. 'Mongolism: When should parents be told'. *Brit. Med. J.*, ii, 1306.

EVANS, K. A., 1962. 'Mentally Handicapped Children'. *Lancet*, i, 974.

FRANKLIN, A. W., 1963. 'Physically Handicapped Babies: Some thalidomide lessons'. *Lancet*, i, 959.

FREESTON, B. M., 1971. 'Caring for a child with Spina Bifida'. Sheffield. Unpublished report for the Association for Spina Bifida and Hydrocephalus.

FREESTON, B. M., 1971. 'An enquiry into the Effects of a Spina Bifida Child upon Family Life'. *Devel. Med. Child. Neurol.* **13**, 456–461.

FORTUNE, T. A., 1962. 'Mentally Handicapped Children: The parents' view'. *Lancet*, i, 161.

GATH, A., 1972. 'The Effects of Mental Subnormality on the Family'. *Brit. J. Hosp. Med.*, August 1972, Vol. 8, No. 2.

GOLDIE, L., 1966. 'The Psychiatry of the Handicapped Family'. *Devel. Med. Child. Neurol.* **8**, 456–462.

HARE, E. H., *et al.*, 1966. 'Spina Bifida Cystica and Family Stress'. *Brit. Med. J.* **2**, 727–760.

HENDERSON, P., 1968. 'The Educational Problems of Myelomeningocele'. *Hosp. Med.*, May 1968, Vol. 2, No. 8.
HEWETT, S., 1970. 'The Family and the Handicapped Child'. Allen and Unwin, London.
HEWETT, S., 1972. 'The Need for Long-Term Care' in: Occasional Papers 2, 3, and 4, Institute for Research into Mental Retardation. Butterworths, London.
JACKSON, *et al.*, 1973. *Community Med.*, 19th January.
JACOBS, J., 1962. 'Mentally Handicapped Children'. *Lancet*, i, 805.
KERSHAW, J. D., 1966. 'Handicapped Children'. Heinemann Medical Books, London.
MACKEITH, R., 1967. 'The Role of a Developmental Paediatrics Centre'. *Med. Biol. Illust.* 1967, **17**, 230–232.
MARTIN, F. M. and REHIN, G. F., 1969. 'Towards Community Care'. Broadsheet No. 508. PEP, London.
MATHENY, A. P. and VERNICK, J., 1969. 'Parents of the mentally retarded child – emotionally overwhelmed or informationally deprived?'. *J. Pediat.* **74**, 953.
MCMICHAEL, J., 1971. 'Handicap – a study of physically handicapped children and their families'. Staples, London.
MEADOW, R. and HEWITT, C., 1972. 'Teaching Communication Skills with the Help of Actresses and Videotape'. *Brit. J. Med. Education* **6**, 317–322.
NATIONAL ASSOCIATION FOR MENTAL HEALTH CONFERENCE REPORT 1964. 'The Whole Truth'. N.A.M.H., London.
NASH, D. F. ELLISON, 1968. 'Spina Bifida and Allied Disorders'. *Hosp. Med.*, January 1968, Vol. 2, No. 4.
ORWELL, S., 1973. 'Handicapped' – summary of Social Policy Research Report. *New Society*, 5th April, 1973, p. 19.
PRECHTL, H. F. R., 1963, for GUNTHER. In: 'Determinants of Infant Behaviour'. Vol. 2, p. 53. Ed. B. M. Foss. Methuen, London.
QUILLIAM, T. A., 1965. 'Clinical Communication – a contemporary problem'. *Med. Bio. Illust.* **15**, 66–68.
THURSTON, J. R., 1959. 'A procedure for evaluating parents' attitudes towards the handicapped'. *Am. J. Ment. Defic.* **64**, 148.
THURSTON, J. R., 1960. 'Counselling parents of the Severely Handicapped'. *Except. Child.* **26**, 351.
TIZARD, J. P. M., 1968. Address to a meeting of the Spastics Society, 25th May, 1968.
WALKER, J. H. THOMAS, M., and RUSSELL, I. T., 1971. 'Spina Bifida and the Parents'. *Devel. Med. Child. Neurol.* **13**, 462–476.
WING, L., 1973. Unpublished data from ongoing research, MRC Social Psychiatry Unit, Institute of Psychiatry, London.
YOUNGHUSBAND, *et al.*, 1970. 'Living with Handicap'. *Nat. Bur. Co-op. Child Care* (now the National Children's Bureau), London.

Paper Five

THE HANDICAPPED CHILD AND THE FAMILY

Hilda Rawlings
Medical Social Worker

Sheila Hewett has provided systematic evidence that many families do not get the help they need. The extreme results of our failures are met in long stay hospitals, children who are there because we have failed to improve professional or practical services to approximate more closely to the needs of their families.

Difficulties for handicapped children and their families are almost always greater than they should be. Interpersonal problems may be identified in marriages and relationships with the handicapped child or other children. External problems are related to finance, inadequate housing, lack of mobility and social isolation, and lack of social and educational opportunities for the handicapped child. Whilst these are co-existent we must accept responsibilities for change and improvement in all directions. Slow progress so far may be due to the reluctance of professions and individuals to cross professional and administrative barriers to achieve proper co-ordination of professional skills for the benefit of these families. Substantial changes in the administrative/political framework are indicated when we know that the lives of many families are being affected by common pressures. One example here is the concern expressed intermittently about the dangers to relationships in the separation of mothers and abnormal babies for purposes of treatment without any constructive moves being made to overcome the problem.

In order to bring about changes at individual, local or national level we must turn first of all to the families. It is their views I try to represent here.

The birth crisis or crisis of diagnosis of handicaps

Many have not experienced sympathetic response to their distress as they would have wished it, or the benefits of 'concretely experiencing reality'[1] at the time of diagnosis.

These situations occur mostly in hospitals where few people seem able to tolerate and share the natural responses of grief, anger, despair, and anxiety. It is especially difficult at birth when mothers are acutely aware of reactions compounded of fear, bewilderment and uncertainty on the part of staff, who may continue to avoid them or isolate them in side wards. On the other hand where doctors have demonstrated concern and humility, without necessarily knowing the answers, parents have felt strengthened and more hopeful.

Staff of maternity and paediatric units might ask themselves to what extent doctors, nurses and others get together to discuss their feelings and reactions to abnormality with a view to establishing a better framework of care. Staff working in stressful situations are themselves vulnerable. Some are naturally able to give support at the critical moment. In the experience of parents this may be a junior nurse or a ward cleaner: it may be a senior doctor.

Training for many young doctors and nurses has not included the chance to study the research by Isobel Menzies[2] or the theory of crisis and work by Gerald Caplan and C. Murray Parkes[3,4,5] who have each described needs in bereavement which prescribe method of care likely to promote mental health rather than ill-health for the individual under stress. The contribution of social work here might be in counselling, if requested, for young nurses and doctors.

Additional needs expressed by families are:

to meet a paediatrician who will give time to a full and realistic appraisal of the medical problem

an early follow-up appointment with the same person and assurance of regular assessment

accessible help day and night where there is an unpredictable medical condition – freedom to telephone a hospital or GP service where there is constant sympathetic attention available (having a telephone within the home may alleviate much unnecessary anxiety)

written information about services available.

Subsequent care

When the child is established within the family the parents want to be involved in care and planning, appreciated for their capacities, and given status in assessment teams. This is their right whether the child is at home or in a hospital or hostel. Where good practice exists parents usually feel able to communicate informally with one member of the team – frequently of their own selection and not necessarily the same person all through – and this individual has the confidence of the whole team. Families want immediate and meaningful response to their signals of distress. This will require much more flexible use of resources. It may be however that a bed overnight in an emergency, or regular week-end breaks for the family, may be preventive of breakdown, whilst waiting lists for long-term care are not. Indeed these are often seen as a threat to make parents keep going, which is punitive.

Parents value highly opportunities for open meeting with staff at hospitals or clinics* – and demands lessen quickly upon doctors who are prepared to meet, with sincerity, any criticisms and complaints which may be part of the exercise.

Voluntary organisation

Similarly by involving themselves in voluntary associations of relatives professional staff have opportunity to demonstrate their commitment and to assess the quality of their own and other services.

The value of shared experiences for many parents is inestimable, yet often overlooked by professional people. This denies to many the compassionate support which may be available in other parents who have experienced similar problems.

Essentially parents wish to be involved and convinced of the effectiveness of our help. Our services should therefore be regarded as extensions to family care. Resources should be available, flexibly and imaginatively, to support them at individual and group level. Where they are not available we should be prepared to work together across professional and administrative boundaries to achieve them. This includes using the maximum capacity of individual families and of voluntary organisations as well as our own. Doctors may have to overcome the traditional expectations of status and superior knowledge. On the other hand social workers and health visitors may have to operate against a general image of themselves which is a poor one.

The complexity of these problems means that no one person can supply the help needed by the family. Effectiveness in our work depends upon multi-disciplinary involvement. Given goodwill and commitment on the part of caring professions better services could be established quickly in the hospital and in the community.

In sustaining families we ourselves are sustained and society is better for the existence of these families. Together we might achieve a more comprehensive service and the relief of stigma and deprivations for the handicapped child and his family.

References
1. Caplan, G. An Approach to Community Mental Health. Tavistock 1961.
2. Menzies, I. The Functioning of Social Systems as a Defence Against Anxiety. Tavistock 1970.
3. Caplan, G. An Approach to Community Mental Health. Tavistock 1961.
4. Caplan, G. Concepts of Mental Health and Consultation. U.S. Dept. of Health Education and Welfare, Children's Bureau 1959.
5. Parkes, C. Murray. Bereavement. Studies of Grief in Adult Life. Tavistock 1972.

* The therapeutic function of relatives' meetings is discussed by Anthony Whitehead: In the Service of Old Age (Pelican), pp. 139–144.

Grateful acknowledgment is made to the parents who participated in the special meeting at Kettering, called to learn of their experiences and to hear their views.

H. RAWLINGS
R. WIGGLESWORTH

Paper Six

PROBLEMS EXPERIENCED BY PARENTS OF CHILDREN WITH SEVERE MENTAL RETARDATION

Lorna Wing
Psychiatrist

Severe mental retardation is a special problem among the abnormalities beginning from birth or very early in life since, in the majority of cases, it cannot with certainty be diagnosed at birth, and can be confirmed only by repeated developmental assessments. Many parents therefore learn that their child is handicapped long after the mother and baby have left the obstetric unit, but the same supporting services have to be mobilised whenever the diagnosis is made.

Emotional and psychiatric symptoms in the parents

A survey of the families of severely mentally retarded children aged 0–14 taken from the Camberwell Register (Wing and Hailey 1972) is being done (Wing 1973a) and an analysis of the first 100 cases is presented here.

The first reaction of the mother on learning that her child was handicapped was often akin to that following bereavement (Hewett 1972). This is an understandable and normal response. In addition to this, 57% of the mothers had had mild or severe psychiatric symptoms at some time since the child was born, mostly anxiety and depression. The numbers with current symptoms (40%) and the numbers receiving treatment from a GP or a psychiatrist during the year before interview, (17%) were very similar to those found for women in general population surveys by Hare and Shaw (1965) and by Shepherd et al. (1966). Nevertheless, 84% of the mothers with symptoms attributed them to the worry of having a handicapped child.

Twenty per cent of fathers had had psychiatric symptoms (including alcoholism) but in only five cases did they feel that this was related to the child.

The reaction of the siblings

There were 248 siblings varying in age from under 1 year to 30 years.

Nine per cent had learning problems, 6% had antisocial behaviour problems and one child only attended a clinic for a neurotic behaviour disorder. More detailed analysis will be needed to show if the siblings had a higher rate of disturbance than the average for Camberwell, but it is clear that the majority did not have overt psychiatric or behavioural symptoms. However, for 23% of all the siblings the parents felt that there were special problems caused by the handicapped child, especially when he or she was aggressive and attacked the brothers and sisters. In less than half of this group the parents reported that the siblings themselves were chronically unhappy and distressed by these problems. For the rest, the parents worried but the siblings seemed to accept the situation.

Attitudes to residential care

One practical measure of the effect of a child on the family is the mother's attitude to residential care. In the Camberwell group 46% felt they had no major current problems with which they could not cope and were happy to have the child at home; 15% had marked problems but still wanted to keep the child; 14% wanted residential care and 25% were living away from the parents (3% with grandparents and 22% in residential care).

The presence of psychiatric symptoms in the mother was not significantly correlated with the attitude to residential care. The factors that were significant were; poor relationship between father and mother; adverse effects upon the siblings; sleepless nights due to the child; disturbed behaviour in the child. These findings are very similar to those of Sheila Hewett (1972).

Sources of practical help and emotional support

The mothers were asked about the help they had received from different services in the past. This was listed under three headings: practical advice on child rearing and behaviour management; help with contacting relevant services; emotional support. The results are shown overleaf. It can be seen that most parents were helped to make contact with appropriate services, but a large proportion received neither practical advice nor emotional support from sources outside the family. Among the professionals the social workers were most often mentioned but the parents noticed a marked lessening of contact with social workers after the social services department was created. The other professionals, including health visitors, were mentioned by only a small proportion of parents. Emotional support from their husbands was mentioned by nearly one third of the mothers.

Analysis of replies by parents

Source of help	TYPE OF HELP		
	Practical advice	Putting in touch with services	Emotional support
No help received	55	15	31
Husband	1	—	29
Other relatives	4	4	23
Other parents	—	4	1
Hospital consultant	11	15	3
G P	4	8	11
Local authority M O	5	5	—
Health visitor	6	17	7
Social worker	10	38	25
Teacher	9	4	4
Other	2	2	5

(*The totals are greater than 100 because some parents mentioned more than one source of help.*)

Discussion

In the group that were studied, the parents, especially the mothers, tended to see the handicapped child as the major source of stress in their lives, although some felt that their child had contributed something positive to the family. Despite the many worries almost half of the families managed the situation very well and even gained from the experience.

The psychiatric problems of the parents were not a significant factor in determining the acceptance of the child. Disturbed behaviour in the child, which was related to specific impairments of cognitive function (Wing 1973b), was clearly one of the major reasons for requesting residential care. Informed advice on child rearing and management of behaviour would have been most helpful but was rarely obtained.

Virtually none of the professional workers in touch with the parents had any knowledge of behaviour management. The situation is now changing for the better with the increasing interest shown by psychologists and their willingness to teach parents how to manage their children. The parents in Camberwell who have been in contact with the recently opened Hilda Lewis Unit are pleased with the help they have received. This does not show in the figures reported because the data was collected retrospectively for 15 years before 1971.

Professional workers who are involved with families when they first learn that they have a handicapped child could try to make an assessment of the problems likely to arise in the future, paying particular attention to those mentioned above. If the stresses and strains could be anticipated some plan could be made to mobilise the positive qualities within the family, especially by emphasising how much they could contribute to their child's development.

On the other hand, if the difficulties were too great, or if the mother and father after a period for consideration felt that they did not want to bring up a handicapped child, then appropriate residential care could be sought in good time instead of in a last-minute crisis.

References

HARE, E. H. and SHAW, G. K., 1965. *Mental Health on a New Housing Estate.* Oxford University Press, London.

HEWETT, S., 1972. The need for long term care in *Occasional Papers No. 2, 3 and 4.* Butterworths, London.

SHEPHERD, M., BROWN, A. C. and KALTON, G. W., 1966. *Psychiatric Illness in General Practice.* Oxford University Press, London.

WING, J. K. and HAILEY, A., 1972. *Evaluating a Community Psychiatric Service. The Camberwell Register* 1964–1971. Nuffield/Oxford University Press, London.

WING, L., 1973a. A survey of severely mentally retarded children and their families in Camberwell (work in progress).

WING, L., 1973b. A study of language impairments in severely retarded children in *Language and Cognition in the Handicapped.* Ed. by N. O'Connor. Butterworths, London, to be published.

Paper Seven

THE ROLE OF THE SPECIALIST IN COMMUNITY MEDICINE IN THE CARE OF HANDICAPPED CHILDREN

Robert Lindon
Elizabeth Harper
Medical Administrators

The future Area Medical Officers and District Community Physicians will be dealing with groups and populations and will therefore be much involved in the planning and provision of services for the handicapped child and his family. In the health districts of the new Area Health Authorities the District Community Physicians will play a vital role in the health care planning teams and one of their number who is a specialist in child health, community paediatrics and school health may be the appropriate co-ordinator of the team of professional workers involved with the family. The suggested brief will be considered in headings:

Watertight administrative machinery

It is suggested that in addition to the computer-based child health record system, a separate handicapped register should be kept centrally in each Area Health Authority. The initial information will come from the birth notification, usually received in the Health Department within three days of child's birth and from the discharge summary giving more details of the handicapping condition.

The register needs to be continuously reviewed by a doctor who is expert in this field if it is to be comprehensive and include details of late diagnosed handicapping conditions. The accuracy of this information, its effectiveness and its appropriate storage on computer will require the services of this doctor supported as necessary by a systems analyst and a computer programmer.

It is essential that there should be close co-operation and communication between medical personnel within the Area Authority if a handicap register is to be made effective.

Choosing the 'teller'

When a handicapping condition is present from birth then it would seem that the best person to tell the parents is the consultant who confirms the diagnosis. This is usually the paediatrician but it may be that he considers that a colleague should do the 'telling'. If the child has an obvious physical handicap the parents seem to accept this more easily as the child remains in hospital for treatment.

From discussions with groups of parents of handicapped children it is apparent that the parents who have a healthy mentally-handicapped child such as a mongol or microcephalic, have found the first two to three weeks most difficult. These children are usually discharged home with mother after one week and it is evident that there is a great need for the community doctor – general practitioner or specialist in community paediatrics – to meet the family in the hospital setting and to visit within a few days of their arrival home. If we envisage a health service where the dichotomy between hospital and community no longer exists, then the 'telling paediatrican' might do the initial home visit.

The long-term supporter

This role might be assumed by one of a number of professional workers. The parent will often choose the long-term supporter as the person with whom she can best communicate. The health visitor and/or social worker have perhaps the best training for this role, but one would envisage regular assessments being done by a team, either in a hospital or community setting, and the decisions as to who is the obvious supporter may vary from time to time.

Specialists in child health community paediatrics and school health

It is recognised that by creating community specialists there is a real danger of perpetuating the dichotomy of hospital and community service. However, one can envisage a paediatrician who works mainly in the community and whose training is in developmental paediatrics and assessment of handicapped children. He will have knowledge of services available for the handicapped child but it is essential that he also has very close links with the hospital in assessment clinics and with the hospital paediatrician. One would hope that the present hospital paediatrician could spend part of his time within the community. The difference between the two being largely one of emphasis.

The community paediatrician would spend most of his time in the schools and units for the handicapped and in the assessment clinics, either in a hospital or community setting. The initial developmental assessments at six weeks and three months are probably best done in the child's home. The parents will be more at ease and the doctor will acquire a better knowledge of the family, the home and some of the problems. It is usually found helpful to have a health visitor present. Later assessments at six monthly intervals can be done in the special clinic provided the atmosphere can be unhurried and informal.

The other members of the team such as the speech therapist or physiotherapist need to be involved early in the case of physical handicap, but with mental handicap the best time may be at the six-month developmental check. The advice before this time can be given by the community paediatrician liaising with his speech therapy and physiotherapy colleagues. Parents should not be confused by the introduction of too many professional workers in the first few months.

Special clinic

Reports on developmental assessments, with recommendations, need to be sent to all professional workers involved with the family, and again the specialist in community paediatrics could be the co-ordinator. His role, relative to the other specialists in community medicine and also in relation to the appropriate education authority, should be clearly set out. Experience leads us to hope that in this particular field there will be a continuance of the mixed clinical and administrative roles similar to those of the present principal medical officer and that the dichotomy between clinical work and administration advocated at present does not take place. There is no doubt whatsoever that administrative recommendations gain immeasurably from the understanding generated by continued clinical involvement.

In Hounslow developmental assessments on mentally handicapped children are done in a special clinic run by a principal medical officer with physiotherapist, speech therapist, health visitor and social worker. The assessments are done at six monthly intervals but the speech therapist and the physiotherapist sees the children more frequently. The doctor and social worker have group meetings with the parents. At the first four or five sessions parents seem to like to chat and share common experiences, but at later sessions talks and group discussions on specific subjects such as language, development, toys, etc. are given. There is feedback from the parents as to what they feel about the service. The table overleaf gives the approximate time spent on this service.

All parents with severely handicapped children suffer severe stress in an acute form when the handicap is recognised and in a more chronic

Estimated time required by community paediatricians for developmental assessments on the mentally handicapped

Estimated numbers of children requiring service	
Child population – (0–15)	43,700
Severely subnormal children (0—15) (3 per 1,000)	138
Newborn diagnosed as ESN (severe)	7–9 per year
Suggested home visits	(2 week, 6 week and 12 week developmental examinations) = 20 per year – 1½ hours each i.e. 30 hours or 10 sessions
Developmental Assessment Clinic (pre-school) (3 children seen per session)	36 children × 2 annually = 72 assessments per year i.e. 72 hours or 24 sessions
School Clinic – (5–16) 4 children seen per session	120 children including 30 special care children 90 children seen annually + 30 children seen 6 monthly = 150 examinations per year i.e. 114 hours – 38 sessions
Administration	40 sessions
TOTAL:	= 112 sessions = 56 days

If the community paediatrician is going to act as the long-term support for some families then many more home visits would be required and time will have to be allowed for new arrivals in the area and also late diagnosed cases. Time will also be spent on discussions with teaching staff.

form of depression and anxiety later. It is important that this is recognised and informal psychiatric screening should be done on all families with handicapped children. The social worker, community paediatrician or health visitor will need to do the screening and refer to a community psychiatrist as it seems unlikely that the health service will have sufficient psychiatrists to provide this service for all parents.

If a dual role as is suggested in this paper is to be given to a specialist in community paediatrics then not only must he be accepted as part of the district paediatric team but also will be held accountable to the Area Medical Officer for that part of his duties which have been clearly delegated to him by the Area Medical Officer or when appropriate by the District Community Physician. In any event if he is to be the co-ordinator of these services he will be in a unique position to supply information on requirements and changing trends on which to base future planning.

Paper Eight

THE EPIDEMIOLOGICAL IMPLICATIONS
affecting the design of a service for the families of handicapped children within the reorganised Health Service

Bernie Spain
Research Psychologist

Since April 1974 the Health Service has been organised on a three-tier basis, with different responsibilities allocated to the Region, the Area and the District. In deciding at which level to locate responsibility for a service, it is hardly necessary to state that the prime criterion must be the welfare of the patient.

Some medical conditions are so rare that a service can only be provided effectively with a large catchment population, while for more common conditions it is more appropriate to provide a service designed to function at a local level. Other considerations which are important are the frequency with which the service is required by the individual patient, the size of the treatment team, and the diversity of disciplines involved in patient care. If the condition is common, if the patient requires treatment frequently, or if the treatment team is large or covers many disciplines whose adequate functioning depends on the ease with which information can be exchanged, then the service must be organized as far as possible at local or District level. Depending on which of these conditions apply, a service for a particular patient group might have to be organised partly through the Area and partly through the District administration.

Considered purely as a problem of epidemiology, the seriously handicapping conditions of childhood can best be discussed in three stages. Firstly, there are those malformations which are immediately apparent at birth or shortly after. Secondly, those which manifest themselves only during the first year or even later, although the pathological lesion or tendency may be present at birth. Thirdly, we need to calculate the proportion of seriously handicapped children from both groups who survive infancy. There will also be a small number who become disabled in the childhood years through post-natal infection or trauma.

All families with a handicapped child will require the same basic service, although the particular personnel involved may vary somewhat depending on the age at which the diagnosis is made, how long the child survives and how successfully the condition can be treated and how severe the handicap.

We now have an abundance of information, derived from various longitudinal studies, on the incidence of seriously handicapping conditions in early childhood. The prevalence of handicap among school-age children is a more complex issue. Somewhat different figures are quoted depending on the criterion for inclusion and on the age at which the children are studied.

Incidence of congenital malformation

It seems fairly well established that within Great Britain between 17 and 18 per thousand total births result in a malformation recognisable within the first four weeks of life and that two-thirds of these, at least, can be detected immediately.[1,2] Many of these children do not survive the neo-natal period and probably over half die within the first year of life.[2,3] Other conditions, however, such as cerebral palsy or severe retardation, due to causes other than mongolism or microcephaly, frequently do not manifest themselves during the neo-natal period, although they may be congenital in the sense that they are due to factors occurring at birth or in embryo.[4]

In studies which trace the progress of children up to school age the overall incidence of handicap, due to factors present at birth or shortly after, approaches 4 per cent[4] (Table 1). This figure includes stillbirths and early deaths as well as survivors to school age. This means that of every birth cohort, about 4 per cent of infants or their families are likely to require special services of some kind at some stage in the child's development because of a handicapping condition, although often the family will require only temporary support, either because the child does not survive or because the condition is mild and can be remedied.

Prevalence of handicap beyond the neo-natal period

In arriving at an estimate of the prevalence of handicap among children over the age of one year, a number of problems arise. Firstly there is the obvious difficulty of estimating survival rates for the congenital malformations. The mortality of children born with a congenital defect is very high in the first six months of life and this is a situation unlikely to change in the future. It is doubtful whether a further reduction in the mortality of such children could now be achieved, even if this were a desirable objective.

Incidence and prevalence of serious handicap detected by seven years (from National Child Development Study)[4]

	Rate per 1,000 live births	Survivors to 7 years per 1,000 7-year-olds
Anencephaly	1·8	—
Spina bifida and hydrocephaly	4·2	1·1
Heart or blood vessels	6·6	3·6
Cleft palate	1·5	1·5
Club feet	4·1	
Dislocated hip	1·1	5·8 (club feet, dislocated hip and other defects of bones or joints combined)
Other defects of bones or joints	2·1	
Other malformations	8·9	2·8
Mongolism	2·0	2·3* (mongolism and other 'severe subnormality' combined)
Other 'severe subnormality'	1·4	
Cerebral palsy	2·5	2·3
Other congenital disorders	2·3	1·9
Cancer, leukaemia and other tumours	0·8	0·2
Total children (some children have more than one defect)	36·6	25·6
Blind or partially sighted (per 1,000 7-year-olds)		1·0
Deaf or partially deaf (per 1,000 7-year-olds)		3·0

* This figure had risen to 3·7 per thousand when the children were followed up to 11 years.

Secondly, some children diagnosed as having a handicap in infancy will be able to receive treatment which will virtually eliminate the problem by the time the child reaches school age, some cases of cleft lip or congenital dislocation of the hip fall within this category.

Thirdly, a child diagnosed, for example as spina bifida or cerebral palsy may have the condition in such a mild form that he cannot be considered to be seriously handicapped. The families of such children may indeed need less advice and support than those of many a non-handicapped child with a sick parent or some other social disadvantage. Similarly, chronic asthma which results in a poor school attendance may be more damaging to a child's educational progress than a mild or well-corrected talipes.

However, there is evidence that even a mild congenital handicap can produce problems, such as behaviour disorders in the child[6] under-achievement at school or maladjustment in the sibs[16] and it would be unwise to assume that such families do not require support.

In consequence of these problems purely methodological issues arise which result in apparently conflicting statistics. Rather different estimates of the prevalence of handicap are given according to the way a study is conducted. One which traces the survival of a cohort of infants with a known congenital malformation will give a different estimate from one which aims to identify the proportion of school children with a chronic physical disorder. There are always some problems in interpreting research findings owing to the inherent limitations of the method chosen. Very large child populations are required to estimate the frequency of the less common disorders, but a study which can accurately assess the degree of handicap suffered and the extent and variety of services required, can only be undertaken on a small number of children because of the time and cost involved.

The National Child Development Study quotes a prevalence of approximately 2.6 per cent in reference to children diagnosed in early life as having a serious or potentially serious handicapping condition and surviving to the age of 7 years.[4] This figure includes some children functioning normally by seven, but it excludes children with a special sensory defect or those with mild or moderate mental retardation or those with chronic conditions such as asthma (Table 1). A study of school children in the Isle of Wight on the other hand puts the prevalence of physical disorder at about 5 per cent.[6] This includes all chronic physical disorder, present during the year previous to the survey count resulting in handicap of some kind, but does not include children with severe subnormality unless this was associated with a physical disorder. The Isle of Wight study suggests however that if one considers all children likely to require some special attention because of chronic educational physical or psychiatric disorder, intellectual retardation or educational backwardness, then this would amount to approximately 14 per cent of children. Educational statistics provide another source of estimate but again using different definitions. They refer only to children receiving or on the waiting list for special education of some kind.[7,8]

Pooling the evidence from all sources it seems safe to conclude that a service for seriously handicapped young children should cater, initially, for an expected prevalence of at least 2 per cent and should include all those with a marked physical or sensory disorder, congenital or acquired, and those who are severely handicapped mentally. Needless to say this is not

Prevalence of handicapping conditions among 9 to 11-year-old children (from Isle of Wight Survey. Table quoted in [14].

	Per 100 children
Educational retardation	7·9
Intellectual retardation	2·6
Psychiatric disorder	5·4
Chronic physical handicap	2·7*
Total with one or more of the above conditions	13·9

* This figure differs from that quoted in ([6]) because of the exclusion of children with a mild physical handicap.

to imply that the medical and social needs of other groups of children, such as those who have mild or moderate retardation, a learning disability, psychiatric disorders or a mild physical handicap are unimportant or require an altogether separate service.

The greatest need is, of course, for a service to cover the needs of children with any physical or mental handicap so severe as to lead to dependence throughout life. If the service were designed *initially* to cater for the needs of those with the more readily identifiable conditions, it could be expanded by degrees to cover all children requiring special help. Ideally, the service should aim to cover any child with a disorder, physical, mental or emotional, although it is not easy to arrive at an accurate estimate of the numbers concerned, and indeed the numbers are likely to vary somewhat throughout the country. Each Area should, in time, be able to build up a register of children with problems which could be used as a basis for planning services.

Population data

Health Districts serve populations of between 150,000 and 500,000. They are grouped to form Area Health Authorities whose size ranges from 200,000 to one million, averaging around 5 or 600,000.

Assuming a live birth rate of 16 per thousand,[10] we would expect in the smaller districts (populations of 200,000) about 3,200 live births and 42 stillbirths each year (a stillbirth rate of 13 per thousand total births).[11] The neo-natal death rate (deaths under four weeks) is approximately 11 per thousand live births and would result in about 35 early deaths.

SPAIN

Approximately 25 per cent of stillbirths and neo-natal deaths are due to congenital malformations[5,14] and most are due to factors evident at birth.[3] Given that the incidence of serious detectable abnormality at birth is 17.5 per 1,000[1,4] then approximately 56 such children would be born each year within the smaller districts. Thirty per cent would be either still-born or die perinatally.

Even in the smaller districts, therefore, there would be at least 100 children each year,* (about two a week) within maternity units either

Approximate number of stillbirths, neo-natal deaths and congenitally malformed school children within a District Health Authority.

	Total population of district	
	200,000	500,000
Number of live births per annum (16 per thousand)	3,200	8,000
Number of stillbirths per annum (13 per thousand total births)	42	105
Deaths under 4 weeks (11·0 per thousand live births)	35	88
	77	193
Congenital malformations		
Diagnosed at birth (1·75% total births)	56	140
Survivors beyond 4 weeks (60%)	35	84
Congenital malformations		
Diagnosed within first year including those diagnosed at birth (3% total births)	96	240
Survivors to one year (50% of those diagnosed under one year)	48	120
Congenital malformations Diagnosed year one to five (1% total births)	32	80
Congenital malformations: total surviving in pre-school years. (Survivors of those diagnosed in the first year, plus those diagnosed year one to five)	48 32 80	120 80 200

* This number is composed of 42 stillbirths, plus 35 early deaths, plus approximately 35 surviving congenital malformations, identifiable at birth.

stillborn or dying from conditions evident at birth or born with a serious and apparent malformation. In a larger district the corresponding number would be about five each week (Table 3). The birth of such a child is not a rare event therefore. It is a quite common occurrence, which warrants an established code of practice and procedure for handling it. Maternity units already provide special facilities for the care of malformed, immature or delicate infants, and each nurse or doctor in the delivery ward is trained to ensure that all babies who require it receive this special care. What we now need to establish is a service, equally well accepted and universal, to cover the needs of the parents during the crisis period immediately following the detection of an abnormality or a perinatal death and which is so designed that an adequate follow-up is guaranteed when the mother leaves the maternity unit. All maternity staff should be taught how to treat parents when this situation arises and how to initiate the service for families. Mothers of stillborn children, those with a child dying in the early weeks, or with a very mildly handicapped child may not require prolonged follow-up. However, they will all require some form of counselling in the early weeks, particularly if the diagnosis carries implications for future pregnancies.

If the progress of all infants is followed regularly during the first year then more handicaps will become apparent. Altogether, including those malformations obvious at birth, over 90 handicapped infants would be identified in the smaller districts and about 240 in the larger ones. Only half of such children will survive beyond the first year, while other handicaps (a further one per cent of total births) will not become apparent till after the age of a year. One might estimate that in the smaller districts there would be about 80 children out of each birth cohort having a serious abnormality, detectable during the pre-school years, and surviving beyond the first year of life.

Since the death rate after the first year is low most of these children and their families will require long term and continuous care. This means that there would be over 300 children (i.e., 80 × 4) between the ages of one and five years, requiring a service. Not every family would need intensive support but all would need information and management advice at least in the early months following the initial diagnosis. These figures are based on estimates for the smaller Districts with a population of 200,000 but one can readily calculate from these the number of families who would be requiring a service in the larger Districts (Table 3). The person most obviously suited to providing domiciliary support and to act as a link between the family and the other services they require is the health visitor.

Staffing considerations and the specialist health visitor

There are 362 consultant paediatricians within the United Kingdom, a ratio of 1:156,000 of the total population,[12] and 646 senior and junior registrars and senior house officers.[13] On average therefore there should be between one and three consultants available within each district depending on its size and two to four senior and junior staff. In addition there were 1,599 full-time doctors in 1972 engaged in school and local authority work, quite apart from the general practitioners or other doctors with part-time clinic appointments,[13] who presumably will be available for work with children within the new structure.

The British Paediatric Association favours rather large in-patient units for children (about 300 beds), in order to ensure efficient care, and only the larger districts will be able to provide the full range of in-patient facilities for children. However, each district hospital is to have a developmental assessment centre, staffed by a multi-disciplinary team, including at least one physiotherapist, teacher, psychologist, occupation therapist, speech therapist and social worker as well as medical, nursing and administrative staff. In some districts there will also be an audiology unit, serving a larger population.

Several members of the multi disciplinary team will have contact with one another in the assessment of each handicapped child since by pooling their expertise they can assess the needs of the child more comprehensively than would be possible if they were working alone. Thus the responsible health visitor must be in touch with three or four or even more members of the team concerning each child. This would hardly be possible unless she herself were a full member of the team, particularly in cases where in-patient facilities are provided at Area or Regional level, because the condition is rare or very complex. The families of children attending such hospitals will be those with the greatest problems and are the very ones most likely to require close hospital-community liaison, but it would seem impossible to maintain adequate contact with the hospital staff unless there was a *specialist* health visitor involved.

At the recommended staffing ratio of 1 to 3,000 population (DHSS Circular 13/72) there would be 66 health visitors practising within a district of 200,000, although in practice the ratio will be closer to 1:7,000 in most areas. The hospital assessment team must meet frequently enough to keep each other fully informed of their findings, and the number of community workers with whom they will work closely must of necessity be limited. It would not be possible for the team to keep in touch with 66 health visitors, or even half that number.

The kind of help a health visitor can give will vary from case to case but it is clearly over practical issues that her help would be most appreciated. There are some problems which arise commonly with a particular diagnosis. For example most parents with a spina bifida child require advice on manual expression of bowel or bladder and the measures needed to avoid severe skin lesions to anaesthetic areas. The best way of coping with incontinence will vary from case to case and therefore close liaison between hospital, health visitor and the family is essential. The handling of cerebral palsied children, teaching them to become independent in association with her hospital colleagues and the adaptation of furniture to meet their needs are matters as practical as they are individual. Unless the health visitor is in close touch with the assessment team she cannot adequately carry out this function. She must be able to consult directly with doctors, occupational therapists, physiotherapists, etc., if she is to ensure that these problems are dealt with as they arise, that no conflicting advice is given and, most important of all, that mothers fully comprehend instructions which are given to them.

If each of the 66 health visitors accepted a general district load she would have responsibility for less than 50 children under the age of one year of whom on average one, or at the most two, would have a serious handicap. She would meet a case of spina bifida at most not more frequently than once in 5 years and perhaps more realistically in 10 years. She would have a case of cerebral palsy on average once in 8 years, a mongol every 10th year and congenital dislocation of the hip once in 20 years. The frequency of contact with these conditions would be slightly higher in a district with fewer health visitors, but there would be no appreciable difference in terms of the amount of experience acquired. Looked at in this way it seems quite unrealistic that one could give all health visitors a course of training which would fit them to give expert and practical support for cases that would come their way so rarely.

Specialist health visitors would be an advantage, therefore, both because of the relative infrequency of handicapping conditions and because of the need for good communication between the health visitor and the hospital staff. Only a specialist health visitor could hope to acquire sufficient knowledge of the full range of handicaps to be of real service to parents and this specialist knowledge would give her the right to participate fully, and as an equal member of the assessment team, making it possible for the staff at the District Assessment Centre to build up a close working relationship with her.

The degree to which the specialist health visitor would accept total responsibility for the day to day care of handicapped children should be decided in each case on its merits. If a district health visitor already has a good relationship with the family it is clearly desirable to work through her if possible. In such cases the specialist health visitor might act solely as a source of information or as a consultant to her non-specialist colleagues. The severity of the disability and degree of expertise required to deal with it or with the family situation are other factors to consider. Children with severe sensory disorders may well require additional domiciliary help from peripatetic teachers, and in some familes special social workers from the district assessment centre might appropriately become the main family contact.

Conclusion

It seems that one cannot hope to produce exact or final figures of the incidence or prevalence of childhood handicap applicable to the country as a whole. The number of children with different conditions will vary both over time and regionally since the incidence of some disorders may differ from year to year or between different parts of the country.[15] Improvements in methods of detection and the spread of facilities for cytology and amniocentesis, etc., will in time affect the incidence of some conditions. The number of children surviving with a handicap will change also according to the treatment methods employed and the facilities available in any one area. Perhaps the most decisive variable of all is the birth rate. The present figures are based on the 1972 estimates of 16.0 per thousand, but this ratio will vary greatly at Area and more especially at District level. Furthermore, the present evidence suggests that we are now witnessing a long-term decline in the birth rate and this is likely to continue as family planning facilities become more readily available.

The most important point for planning however is to indicate the *order* of figures involved – will there be tens or hundreds or thousands of handicapped children within an Area health authority? Clearly there is enough material available to make this sort of estimate and while one might argue with details of the figures presented here, they should be accurate enough as a starting point for establishing a service.

The same limitations apply to some extent to the figures quoted of the number of personnel available. These numbers are not fixed and will vary both nationally and locally depending on the number of basic training places available and on the incentives given for post-graduate training and also how many schemes exist for in-service training or refresher courses. There are at present, of course, big regional variations in the number of professional staff, (especially in the non-medical staff) available, but it might be possible to produce a more equal distribution of resources by a deliberate policy of incentives to work in the less well endowed areas.

Greater local autonomy and the opportunity one might gain to put new ideas into operation might in fact prove a much greater pull in this respect than any financial rewards.

Given these provisos, however, the present figures clearly imply that in organising a service for handicapped children and their families it would be appropriate to focus the service at the District level. Handicapping conditions are quite common enought to warrant it although children with rarer conditions might have to be under consultant care at the Area or even Regional level. Even in cases where much of the in-patient care has to be undertaken at Area or Regional level it should still be possible to provide some out-patient facilities locally, at the District General Hospital. Most of these children require continuous medical attention at least in the pre-school years, and therefore it would be preferable to organise medical and support services locally, as far as possible, especially since many disciplines will be involved in the care of the child and his family.

Domiciliary services must necessarily be organised on a district basis. Health visitors with a specialist training could most efficiently provide the skilled practical advice which families need and also act as a link between the home and the hospital personnel involved in the child's care. The siting of the hospital clinics is not the most relevant issue, it is the absence of effective liaison between hospital departments and medical and nursing staff in the community which produces many of the existing problems. It is essential to overcome the present situation where the exchange of information between those involved in treatment, education and family care is commonly so inadequate. A service which is organised, as far as possible, at District level, with specialist health visitors, should facilitate contact between the members of the treatment team and so help to eradicate the present dichotomy between hospital and community.

References

1 McKeown, T. and Record, R. G., 1960, 'Malformations in a population observed for five years after birth'. In Ciba Symposium on Congenital Malformations. Ed. G. E. W. Wolstemholme and C. M. O'Connor, Churchill.
2 Butler, N. R. and Alberman, E. 1969. 'Perinatal Mortality Survey. Livingstone.
3 McKeown, T., 1965. 'Medicine in Modern Society'. George Allen and Unwin.
4 Davie, R., Butler, N. and Goldstein, H., 1972. 'From Birth to Seven'.
5 Grundy, F. and Lewis-Faning, E., 1957. 'Morbidity and Mortality in the First Year of Life'. Eugenics Society.
6 Rutter, M., Tizard, J. and Whitmore, K., 1970. Education, Health and Behaviour'. Longman.
7 'The health of the schoolchild 1966–68'. Report of the Chief Medical Officer of the Department of Education and Science (1969), HMSO.

SPAIN

8 'Statistics of Education' (1972) 1971, Vol. 1, Schools. Department of Education and Science, HMSO.

9 National Health Service Reorganisation: England (1972). HMSO Cmd. 5055.

10 Annual Abstract of Statistics, 1972. No. 109, Central Statistical Office, HMSO.

11 Registrar General Statistical Review of England and Wales for the year 1970. Part II Tables, Population, POCS, HMSO.

12 COURT, D. and JACKSON, A., Ed., 1972. 'Paediatrics in the Seventies'. OUP, Nuffield Provincial Hospitals Trust.

13 CHAMBERLAIN, R. M., 1972. 'Children in the Integrated NHS'. *The Lancet*, Vol. II, pp. 963–965.

14 TIZARD, J., 1974. 'The epidemiology of handicapping conditions of educational concern'. Chapter in Pringle, K. M. and Vavina, V. P. (Eds.). *Advances in Educational Psychology*. London University of London Press.

15 TEW, B. and LAURENCE, K. M., 1973. Mothers, Brothers and Sisters of Patients with Spina Bifida'. *Developmental Medicine and Child Neurology*. Suppl. No. 29, Vol. 15, No. 6, pp. 69–76.

RIGHT FROM THE START

A service for families with a young handicapped child.

Bernie Spain
Guy Wigley *Editors*

Section Two

Discussion based upon the eight papers presented in Section One.

This section summarises the points made during the discussion session of a Symposium held in London on May 4th, 1973, sponsored by Medical Department, GLC/ILEA.

Chairman **Ronald MacKeith**

Contents Discussion points
Recommendations for the setting up of a service within the framework of the reorganised National Health Service.

List of Participants

Abstract from: Right from the Start
ISBN 0 855 37027 0
Published by NSMHC 1975 Price £1.25
Pembridge Hall Pembridge Square
London W2 4EP

Additional copies of the full text, and this abstract can be obtained from NSMHC, Pembridge Hall, Pembridge Square, London.

Price £1.25 Full text Price of Summary 20p

The following organisations which were represented by observers at the Symposium wish to be associated with this report and with the purpose which lay behind its production.

The Association for Spina Bifida and Hydrocephalus
The Invalid Children's Aid Association
The King Edward's Hospital Fund for London
The Lady Hoare Trust for Physically Disabled Children
The National Society for Mentally Handicapped Children
The Spastics Society

DISCUSSION SUMMARY

The Problem

1 The discovery either at birth or later in infancy that a child has a mental or physical handicap is by no means a rare event, and it is one which places great strain on the family. It follows that the provision of a suitable programme of care for the child and his family warrants serious consideration. There are two aspects to this problem; first, the urgent and crucial matter of how best to break the news to the parents; secondly, how best to supply the emotional and practical support which families are likely to need, in the years to come. The evidence suggests that on both counts we are failing markedly at present to provide the kind of service which families require.

2 No matter how well or badly the situation is handled, many parents will make a reasonable adjustment, but they will often have suffered unnecessarily in the process. A few will break with the strain of having a handicapped member, however well and sympathetically they are supported. But undoubtedly there is a high proportion who could make a good adjustment to the situation, if properly helped, but who will otherwise fail in some vital respects.

3 Adjustment has many facets, first it involves accepting the handicapped child as he is, appreciating his abilities rather than concentrating on his disabilities; secondly, giving the child neither more nor less than his rightful place in the family; thirdly, recognizing the effect the handicapped child may have on his parents and on his brothers and sisters and minimising the strain this may impose upon them; and finally, but of course equally important, ensuring that the child himself achieves his potential and becomes as independent as possible. Making a good adjustment can only come about very slowly and places great demands on the parents and they are likely to need help. In the beginning they need to be encouraged to admit to the ambivalent and negative feelings which they invariably have. Failure to

admit to and come to terms with these feelings, early on, is likely to cause problems later.

4 Failure to adjust to the situation may produce emotional ambivalence or rejection, and at worst the child may be abandoned. It may also result in an excessive focusing of activities and interests around the handicapped child, with detriment to other family relationships, and the legitimate needs of the brothers and sisters. Nor does it help the handicapped child himself if he is understimulated or overprotected. Sometimes parents quite rightly decide that the child requires residential care, because the family is unable to function with the child at home, and they need help in reaching this decision also. The overall objective must be to enable the handicapped member to live as normal and independent a life as is compatible with his degree of disability, and the welfare of others. This can only be achieved when the family has learnt to accept his presence and to appreciate his personality and achievements, and also to recognise what limitations to his and their lives are implied by his handicap.

5 There is good evidence to show that a high proportion of parents consider that they are not being given the consideration and help they require to achieve this. Many feel that the news was broken to them with insufficient sensitivity or opportunity for discussion, despite the fact that it is accepted generally that this is a critical interview. Furthermore, they claim that they are given little practical advice or emotional support from sources outside the family.

6 It is frequently said that because of the parents' natural distress when they first learn of the handicap, they do not remember the help and support given to them. It must be acknowledged that the parents' recollection of that interview will often be seriously faulty because of their distress, and indeed it may take months or even years for them to fully comprehend what has happened. But the doctors and the other professionals concerned have met this situation before. They must recognise fully that parents may not immediately appreciate the full implications of the diagnosis, and they must take this fact into account. One cannot escape from the conclusion that it is the professionals who hold the responsibility for ensuring that the salient facts are communicated, and communicated sympathetically. When large numbers of parents of handicapped children are seriously critical of the initial telling and of the practical and emotional support which they have received, we must accept that the present services are failing to satisfy a legitimate need. There is no shortage of medically supported anecdotal evidence to confirm the parents' view.

7 Undoubtedly a great barrier to the provision of a good service up to the present has been the clumsy and divisive nature of health service organisation and the unfortunate split between community and hospital services. With the advent of reorganisation we have before us the opportunity to reconsider the needs of families with a handicapped child, and having decided what it is that they require, we must then devise an organisational framework which will be conducive to the emergence of the service which they desire to see.

The discovery of the defect

8 What should be said and done will depend on many things. One important factor is whether the handicap is obvious at birth or whether it is not so obvious, especially to parents, but capable of diagnosis by skilled examination shortly after birth. By far the largest group are those which only manifest themselves months or years later such as mild or moderate mental retardation and most cases of cerebral palsy and disorders of hearing and vision.

9 Today nearly all babies are born in hospital and their mothers are but rarely under general anaesthesia for delivery. Many, perhaps most, mothers experience the fear at some time during pregnancy that the baby may be born deformed in some way. During the ante-natal examination the examining doctor should be alert for oblique references as well as direct mention of this possibility and be prepared to make available time for sympathetic discussion. Where there is an unusually high possibility of such an occurrence the doctor will carefully consider whether he should take the initiative in raising the subject.

If the mother is at risk for an abnormal birth because of an abnormal pregnancy or previous obstetric history then the paediatrician could be warned in advance, told of the expected date of delivery, and consulted about the handling of the immediate birth situation, should the child be born handicapped. If the obstetrician is present at the birth then of course he will be the first person to speak to the mother.

9 Unless a defect is at once apparent, the mother will be expecting the midwife or the obstetrician to assure her that all is well. If she understands, from ante-natal training, that a thorough examination by the paediatrician is always routinely carried out but that this cannot usually be done on the spot, she will accept some comment such as 'the baby seems to be all right'. As soon as possible, and certainly within 24 hours, the paediatrician should examine the child for any hidden defect.

11 The situation is quite different of course where the abnormality is immediately detectable at birth. Because the moment of birth is a very emotional one and everyone hopes for a healthy child, doctors and nurses are often over-reassuring. It is especially important not to give the mother the impression that some observed abnormality is trivial when it is not. If an obvious defect is present then the senior member present must decide whether to speak of it immediately or delay the telling for some hours. A tired mother at the emotional moment of birth is not prepared for bad news, but she may have seen the meningocele on her child, or noticed the look on the face of the midwife at the moment of birth, and her queries must then be dealt with immediately.

The handling of such situations needs long experience, understanding and tact and will vary in individual situations. It is helpful for paediatric and obstetric departments to hold periodic discussions between all the staff involved, so that the many problems can be appreciated and the individual professional workers equipped as well as possible to deal with the situation they may encounter. They must be guided by one golden rule; a lie must never be told, nor a half lie based on hope not on knowledge. Doctors and nurses should be encouraged to face these problems during training and may need continuous support if they experience particular difficulty over this issue.

12 Parents almost all agree that they think it right to be told without significant delay, but if the matter can be left long enough – a matter of hours only – it becomes possible to use a more planned approach. In such a situation some paediatricians prefer to speak first to the husband and ask him if he wishes to tell his wife himself, or to be present while the paediatrician tells her. Many experienced in this field consider the mother can often take the initial blow better than the father. Many think that the mother or father should be holding the baby at the moment they are told.

In deciding on a course of action in each individual case the background and character of the individuals concerned, so far as these are known, and the multiplicity of factors influencing the decision should be recognised.

13 Both parents must be told the facts fully and quickly, but where it is possible, the news may be given in several stages. If the mother is too drugged at the time of birth to comprehend what has happened, then she must be seen again on awakening and not left to try to piece together what she was told earlier. It should not be left to one parent to inform the other what has happened unless this is a specific request.

Once they have heard the diagnosis the parents need a place where they can express grief privately. There is no substitute for insightful knowledge of the family such as may be held by the family doctor or the health visitor. It is in any case particularly important to inform the family doctor as soon as the defect is discovered, since he may well be approached by other members of the family for information and advice.

14 In no circumstances should the early discussions with the parents be left entirely to junior doctors or nurses, who may not have sufficient knowledge, training or experience to handle the situation with the skill and tact required. But they need to know what the mother has been told and how to get further help in answering parents' questions. Whenever or however parents are told about the baby the most senior nurse on the ward should also be present at the interview so that she may inform her colleagues. When the doctor has gone it is to the nursing staff that the mother will most likely turn for information as questions occur to her. It is vital therefore that the nurses should know what the mother has been told, and what they in turn should say. If the mother turns to the younger nursing staff for further reassurance or information then the senior members of staff should acknowledge this choice and support her in every way necessary. At this stage the medical social worker should be involved so that she can help the parents and the staff to accept the situation.

15 No one would dispute that good informal communication between the medical and nursing and social work staff help to make a good maternity or paediatric unit, and if the paediatrician is easily accessible then nurses and social workers can discuss the diagnosis with him and feel free to talk to the mother, as the situation demands. This is especially important if the baby has been transferred to another hospital, when the mother will rely on the nurses to keep her informed about the baby's progress (though such a special unit should, wherever possible, be sited near enough for the mother to continue to have access to her baby). It is very distressing for mothers if people are evasive, since this is seen to indicate lack of sympathy or disinterest. Nurses should not feel constrained by lack of information or fear of reprimand. The problem is no different of course from that encountered on any hospital ward, since patients often wish to discuss their treatment and prognosis with nurses. But in this particular case it is more than usually important that nurses do not appear to prevaricate, since this will aggravate the mother's worst fears, add to her confusion, and is likely to precipitate fantasies whose horrors may far exceed the reality. All doctors and nurses, however junior, should be

coached in and given practice in dealing with this sort of situation. Drama techniques in which students deal with simulated situations with professional actors could be more widely used to sensitise people to these problems early in their careers.

16 Whether the breaking of the news is fully planned or not the emotional anguish of the parents is such that frequently the information is not properly understood or remembered however sympathetic and skilled the teller may be. At least two or three sessions are usually required before the parents can comprehend the diagnosis. It may be best to follow up any important interview with another from a different person, another paediatrician or a social worker, who asks 'what were you told' to elicit the parents' perception of the situation. It is sometimes said that consultants are too busy for such time-consuming repetition but a judgment as to whether sufficient time is available essentially involves a question of priorities. Where it is appreciated that this is a matter of great importance, it will be accorded high priority, whatever the other calls on the doctor's time.

17 It is necessary to explain to both parents as early as possible what genetic factors may be present, and in all cases to emphasise that the child's condition is no-one's fault and that neither parent is to blame. Family planning advice is essential always, but especially if there are genetic factors, and the initiative for seeking these things should not be left to the parents, since they may be too pre-occupied with the immediate problems to think of the future. The emotional and sexual relationship between the parents may be very delicate at this time with anxiety about the cause, and the worry of possibly having another abnormal child, but the need for mutual comfort is perhaps greater than at any other point in their marriage. One's concern must be for the implications this situation has for the future marital integration, as well as for the needs of the moment. More than one approach may be necessary and the paediatrician, social worker, health visitor and general practitioner should all feel a responsibility in ensuring that the parents do understand any genetic factors and are making use of whatever family planning services are required.

Continued care

18 The family with a handicapped child will need someone who can, from his or her special knowledge, give the necessary guidance and who will be available when the parents want such help. This main supporter need not necessarily be the same person, partly because the needs of each situation will vary, but the various aspects of the care of

anyone with a continuing handicap need to be integrated, and one person must accept the responsibility for achieving this. In the first few years after a baby or a young child has been recognised as handicapped, this person should be the District paediatrician. While the newborn child is in hospital, the parents will discuss with him the baby's present and future.

19 When the baby goes home the family doctor, the health visitor and community child health physician will then become involved. Of necessity most family doctors will have little experience of all the complex problems posed by handicapped children, although the day to day medical care will, of course be provided by him. Guidance on bringing up the child will be provided by the health visitor and Community Child Health Physician, (the latter may sometimes in fact be the child's general practitioner).

20 The specialised overall care of the handicapped child will be provided by the District centre for assessment and care, a part of the Children's Department of the District General Hospital. On the staff will be the paediatrician and a community child health physician, especially appointed to help handicapped children. It would also be appropriate to attach to the District Assessment Centre, a health visitor specialising in the needs of handicapped children and their families, who would act in association with the child's general practitioner and the local health visitor. The specialist health visitor, the social worker from the district assessment centre and the community child health physician would undertake regular home visiting to provide the support and guidance needed between periodic visits to the paediatrician at the district assessment centre, or in the out-patient department.

21 It must be recognised that however conscientious the paediatrician, or however deep his concern for the parents, he may not be able to act as the main supporter indefinitely. It is extremely important that, on the staff of the District Assessment Centre, there should be a person of special skill, experience and sympathy available to take on this role. She should be introduced to the mother by the doctor before mother and baby leave the hospital. She must be acknowledged as a full member of the child health care team, for if she is to develop and maintain expertise then she will need to have contact with and hold the confidence of the other members of the team. We suggest that a specially trained health visitor would be the most appropriate person for this task, since she, having a nursing training, can cover the medical aspects of the child's condition, as well as giving more general advice on child care and management.

22 The role of the specialist health visitor would be to provide assistance in the pressing practical problems of infant and child care, complicated by an abnormality, and helping the parents to play a positive role in encouraging the child's development, so that they have the satisfaction of active participation. She could ensure that the parents were fully informed about the child's progress and his current and future developmental needs, referring them for specialist help when necessary, and ensuring that they are seen periodically at the District Assessment Centre. She would form an important channel of communication between the child's family and the staff of the specialised paediatric unit and the developmental assessment centre, provided as part of the Children's Department of the District General Hospital. She could help in making the necessary links between the family, the hospital, the education and social services departments and with whatever voluntary bodies were concerned. She could therefore keep the parents informed about what facilities were available to them locally, at the hospital, through the social services department, or later in the school to help them cope with problems the handicap brings. She could also provide information about the local voluntary organisations which exist and provide special facilities, for example, toy libraries, pre-school playgroups and other supporting services for families.

25 Almost certainly, frequent discussions will be required before the parents can make a realistic appraisal of the child's future potential, and parents usually find it helpful to do this in part in their own homes. In this setting some of the practical problems of management and training may be resolved more swiftly. A health visitor with special training could provide the mother with this sort of domiciliary service, and could feed back information about home conditions to the paediatric unit or assessment centre, which is essential for the understanding of the child's problems. Having access to the child's case-notes and to the consultants she could amplify explanations about the condition or of the treatment, when the mother asks for this, and she could attend out-patient clinics with the mother so as to form a real bridge between community and hospital services. Where her expertise is inadequate in any particular case, she could call on her colleagues, the social worker, the psychologist, the occupational therapist. Parents do not always realise that such disciplines exist, nor the help that they can provide, and therefore cannot by themselves seek help when it is needed. The social worker attached to the paediatric unit or assessment centre, would work closely with the health visitor, especially where the marital relationship was poor, or where the

mother was not coping well for some other reason. Indeed, in par ticular cases it may be appropriate for the social worker to take the lead role. The important fact to recognise is that each worker has a special contribution to make and that they work in co-operation in all cases.

24 Parents with a handicapped child rarely have previous experience of the problems that handicap brings. If it is a first-born child, they do not even have experience of normal child rearing. They are at risk for some obvious emotional pitfalls – obvious to the professionals who have worked with other families, but not so obvious to the parents. There are certain faulty behaviour patterns which can develop in relation to the child, or the other family members which are common in such families and which could perhaps be prevented from flourishing if they were discussed openly and frankly. There are many common problems in child rearing, distressing eating or sleeping habits, temper tantrums, etc., which can be alleviated by behaviour modification techniques, if parents can be taught how to apply these methods. At present parents get little help in these areas, but a specialist health visitor (supported by the psychologist) working largely within the home, could help the mother to deal with these common problems or refer her for specialist help where necessary.

25 Parents need to learn something about normal child development, physical, intellectual and emotional, so that they can observe for themselves what stage the baby has reached and know what is appropriate to help him reach the next stage. This is especially important for parents with a mentally handicapped child who get little community help at present. The practical task of identifying and providing for the child's developmental needs will involve additional workers such as psychologists and occupational therapists, working partly on a domiciliary basis, as well as playgroup leaders and teachers.

26 The range of conditions to be encompassed by the specialist health visitor would be a matter for local discussion. Special training would be required within centres of excellence up and down the country as well as instruction within the local paediatric unit and assessment centre.

27 The mother may of course choose her own special confidant. If she makes a better relationship with her family doctor, the social worker or physiotherapist, then this should be allowed to develop and information can be channelled through this person. There is no room for adherence to rigid professional boundaries when the welfare of the

child is involved, and if the mother finds it easier to talk to one person then her choice should be respected.

The family doctor

28 When a child with obvious congenital deformities is born in hospital the general practitioner is not immediately involved but he should be put fully in the picture at least by the time mother and child are discharged home. He may well be invited to see the mother while still in the maternity unit, or consulted by telephone about the initial interview with them. The paediatrician should not only acquaint him with the medical facts and their implications but explain what the parents have been told and how they re-acted. It is highly desirable that a member of the district assessment team, be it health visitor, social worker or community child health physician, should supplement this information with a face-to-face talk with the family doctor; without this full briefing he cannot contribute a supportive role; and the help he is able to give throughout childhood will depend on a close working relationship with the district assessment team and particularly with the health visitor and the social worker.

29 Where the realisation that the child is not normal emerges little by little, the family doctor bears a heavy responsibility. When the general practitioner does not himself undertake systematic developmental examinations he should be kept informed by the child health physician of any disturbing findings and the implications in terms of services and support made clear.

It is where the mother herself experiences misgivings concerning the normality of the child's development, that the family doctor should be especially vigilant particularly if he is not himself trained in the techniques of developmental assessment.

Reassurance based simply upon a desire to comfort is dangerous and often harmful. Parents who express unease must be listened to seriously, since they are often proved to be right. If there appears to be any developmental delay then the child should be referred for full assessment at the district assessment centre.

30 Genetic counselling will often be given by the hospital consultant. Always the nature of this advice and how it was received should be transmitted to the family doctor. Siblings may sometimes need genetic advice but find it difficult to ask their parents, and grandparents may on occasion need explanations about the child's condition and the genetic implications. These functions may be best carried out by the family doctor. Where parents consult him about recurrence risk,

the GP should refer them to a genetic counsellor for specific advice on this point since reassurance without foundation may be disastrous. The memorandum 'Human Genetics' issued by the Department of Health and Social Security is very helpful in this regard and should enable the family doctor to deal with most queries which are likely to arise.

31 The role that the general practitioner plays will vary according to circumstance. Where he knows the family, then he is usually consulted by the parents either for further explanations or for mobilising help from others. In all cases he has an important role to fulfill and to achieve this he must have full information about the child and his treatment, and long-term plans for continued care. In situations where the family doctor feels unable to deal with a problem then he may decide to ask for help elsewhere and in this case, of course, he must know where to find it. Again the help of the specialist health visitor as co-ordinator of information at the local level would be invaluable to the family doctor, especially where the child suffers from some condition rarely encountered in a general practice.

Facilities provided through the Joint Consultative Councils

32 Through the Joint Consultative Councils, now being set up in each health area, it should be possible to produce joint plans with the Social Services and Education Departments. The provision of local boarding facilities for handicapped children should be a priority for the JCCs. Not all families can undertake full-time care of their handicapped child, especially as he grows older and heavier and more difficult to manage. Although often at present this is the only alternative available, few parents willingly give consent for their child to go into permanent institutional care, especially since most residential establishments are too far away for frequent visiting.

33 The provision of small residential units within the community where children can board weekly or live throughout most of the year would encourage the maintenance of ties between the child and his family, when he can no longer be cared for entirely at home. These units could also offer temporary relief to families during a crisis period, such as when another baby is born or if one of the other children is taken into hospital, or simply when the parents feel the need for a short rest. For parents of the mentally handicapped child, the provision of short-stay hospital care has become a highly valued service over recent years, but most parents would prefer the child to be placed locally, and if possible not within a hospital, bearing as it must, all the

connotations of treatment and distress. The mere *knowledge* that this type of temporary relief was readily available locally, and without all those disturbing aspects associated with a formal hospital admission, would be beneficial in itself.

34 Parents availing themselves of this service need not feel the guilt often attached to the idea of 'putting my child away'. It must be frankly recognised that in some cases disturbance among the siblings and marital disharmony can only be alleviated by temporary, weekly, or even permanent residential care for the handicapped member, and there should be no shame attached to this choice or no implication that, because residential care is sought, the parents have therefore rejected their child.

35 Another important area for the Joint Consultative Councils to discuss should be the provision of pre-school education facilities. There is need for a variety of provision, peripatetic teachers, day nurseries and play-groups. It is obviously an advantage if these can be developed in consultation with the team at the district assessment centre and if the work of peripatetic teachers can be co-ordinated with that of the specialist health visitor.

Communications

36 An efficient but sensitive network of communications is needed both within the district assessment centre or paediatric unit, and between it and the many agencies in the community who are also involved in the child's care. Each person concerned should know the functions and limitations of the others and should feel that each complements the other. The responsibility for seeing that good communication is achieved should rest with the Area Specialist in Community Medicine (Child Health) and his colleague at district level, the Community Child Health Physician, who will be a member of the district paediatric assessment team. They would be responsible for ensuring good communications within the team and with outside agencies.

37 The parents will set great store on the advice they receive when they visit the assessment unit and the support received by the family is not simply a matter for the specialist health visitor and social worker but for the assessment/caring team as a whole. Yet at any moment in time it must be possible to say which member has prime responsibility for family support. As time goes by this may pass from one member of the team to another according to the activities undertaken in relation to the child, with different individuals playing a more or less prominent

role at different points in time. The parents' feeling towards members of the team must be taken into account. Effective support requires a relationship between supporter and supported and this in turn involves listening to the parents with an ear sensitive to what hopes or anxieties lie behind the actual words used.

38 Full respect should be accorded to the parental role in the care of these children. It is essential that medical information be shared with them and that parents be given confidence in their own ability to cope. Parents commonly can and do cope exceedingly well, but they usually need some professional help and support. An effective therapeutic team must develop the capacity for support, always recognising that the most important members of the team are the parents themselves. Traditionally the dialogue has been one-way, but parents' observations and comments are at least as valuable as those of the professionals and they must be encouraged to feel that this is accepted by everyone. If they are reassured that they are doing a good job, then they will have the self-confidence to carry on, to make suggestions and ask questions.

39 Clearly, telling the parents the facts concerning their child's condition and giving practical and sympathetic support during the pre-school years are tasks both complex and delicate. The telling process calls for patience, repetition and above all for perceptive listening to what the parents have to say. Often their deepest anxieties are not obvious and may only be revealed to a sympathetic and sensitive listener.

The role of the family and the local community

40 This document has so far concentrated on organisational factors, or the functions appropriate to different professional groups. This is inevitable since its intention is, primarily, to discuss an improved administrative framework for caring for the handicapped child. But this emphasis should not be interpreted as a belief that only the 'experts' have a contribution to make to this problem.

41 Many people have suggested in fact that the major defect in the present service is the failure to recognise the central role which is played by the *family* in the care of such children. Little effort is made to involve anyone except the mother in discussions of the child's treatment and prognosis, and few direct attempts are made to mobilise aid within the family or the local community to assist and support the mother in her task.

42 The father, of course, is the person whose interest and involvement must be elicited and encouraged from the start, especially if it appears that he is not the kind of father who automatically accepts equal responsibility with his wife for the care of their offspring. It should be made clear that his presence at the out-patient clinic is just as vital as the mother's and financial assistance should be found to enable him to take time off work when necessary, if his firm fails to provide this. He needs to understand the developing child's needs and his educational prognosis just as clearly as the mother. Domiciliary visits at a time when he can be present should be arranged from time to time, so that the specialist health visitor doctor or social worker can see both parents together, on home territory, giving them the opportunity to discuss their child's progress and any problems which either of them feel are being overlooked. No professional person however sympathetic or talented can equal the support that a concerned father can give to the child and the mother. It follows that it must be the prime aim of the service to foster paternal participation. Medical social workers, of course, do appreciate this but they must be supported by their other colleagues.

43 Other members of the family, grandmothers, aunts, cousins may also be willing to help, provided that they are given the necessary encouragement to do so. It is rarely at present pointed out to them that their participation, be it only the occasional baby-sitting, can make an important contribution to maintaining family relationships and easing the emotional burden on the parents. The specialist health visitor or the social worker, with the co-operation of the general practitioner, could contrive to ensure that this idea was conveyed to other members of the family, so that the initiative was not left entirely with them nor with the mother.

44 In cities close relatives often do not live near enough to make a contribution, but we tend, in our society, to underestimate the goodwill of neighbours, and nowhere is this more apparent than in the case of the handicapped child. The specialist health visitor should initiate and develop local groups for parents with handicapped children, so that they can meet regularly to discuss emotional problems and offer each other practical support in terms of experience, equipment and baby sitting. But there is no reason whatsoever to exclude the rest of the community. Housewives with grown children, students, sixth-formers and those who are retired but still active and healthy will often welcome the opportunity to contribute to the care of handicapped children in practical ways, such as helping to run a playgroup, taking the handicapped child out occasionally, driving the car-less parent and

child to the out-patient clinic; caring for the other children for a few hours or doing a bit of shopping or cooking to help parents visiting a child in hospital.

45 There would, of course, be direct financial advantages to the health and social services if the local community were encouraged to help in such ways. But most important of all would be the knowledge the parents would gain that they were not alone in their struggles, and the confidence that the child, although deformed, was found to be lovable and acceptable to those outside the family circle. Where the natural sympathy of the family, neighbours and the local community can be developed to augment or replace professional services, this can help the disabled child to feel more 'normal', more accepting of himself and more at ease in the company of others.

The need for an administrative framework

46 An effective service for families with a handicapped child is formed of a complex network of personnel and services and it will not come into being automatically. *Possibly the main reason why a good service does not exist at present is the fact that there is no-one designated with overall responsibility for seeing that parents do receive the help that they need.* It requires first, of course, that all concerned clearly see the value of this service and are prepared for the effort involved in initiating it. *But, given that, someone also has then to assume the responsibility for bringing the different professions together to discuss how the service can best be organised, given local circumstances.* He will need to lead detailed discussions concerning the role of individual members of the team and what is necessary to ensure full and free communication between them.

47 Everyone concerned should know that there is a particular person responsible for the overall organisation of a co-ordinated service for families with a handicapped child. Within the new structure the appropriate person to do this would be the Area Specialist in Community Medicine (Child Health) together with the District Community Physician. Some parts of the service will presumably be organised at Area level, for example, specialist in-patient or assessment facilities and while others, like the health visitors, would operate at the district level. It would be necessary, in some form or another, to bring together both medical and nursing staff of the obstetric and paediatric teams together with community workers such as health visitors and social workers who would be involved in the care of the handicapped child and his family. The aim would be to evolve a policy for that Area and for each District within that Area.

48 In their discussion these people would decide:

(a) who in each maternity unit would be responsible for telling the parents initially that the child was handicapped and what steps that person should then take to ensure adequate follow-up;
(b) how a co-ordinated service could best be organised within that Area and within each District and what should be the function of each member of the team.

A clear understanding of the importance of communication between members of the basic treatment team, and between them and others outside, such as GPs, would be essential for an efficient system, and a detailed specification should be produced about who must be informed in any particular circumstances.

49 The organisation would of course have to be updated from time to time but the group decision should be committed to paper. A copy should go to all concerned and care taken to see that new staff joining the team receive this. The document would be particularly important for junior staff, for it would help them to develop the correct attitudes to this problem early in their professional life.

50 It is essential that parents also know how services are organised and the different people who will be involved in the child's care. They should also receive printed information explaining the procedure and with key names, addresses and telephone numbers, so that they can easily make enquiries when any particular problem arises.

Summary of recommendations

1 In every case of congenital abnormality recognised at birth one member of the hospital staff must assume responsibility for telling the parents and initiating long-term support.

2 The person concerned may vary from case to case according to circumstances, but usually it will be the paediatrician who will play the leading role.

3 All professions involved in the care of the mother and child should feel involved in supporting the parents. Their efforts should be co-ordinated by the paediatrician, but flexibility is desirable so that a mother's attachment to a particularly sympathetic member of the staff may be fostered.

4 There must be available as a full member of the multi-disciplinary team caring for the child, a health visitor whose role is to give practical help,

advice on child management and long term support on a domiciliary basis. She should be introduced to the parents by the paediatrician soon after the diagnosis is made. This long-term role will take up much of her time since she must be a person of some expertise and would need to have the time available for frequent contacts with the children's unit. There is need too for the secondment of a social worker to join the team as a permanent member. But this does not mean that the other members of the (hospital-based) treatment team need no longer be concerned with support. Children diagnosed as having a serious abnormality at any time during the pre-school years will also require the services of the specialist health visitor. The doctor diagnosing the child should initiate this service.

5 The general practitioner will have a particularly important role to play and will often be able to give the paediatrician background information about the home and family circumstances as well as providing long-term support. A practitioner cannot be expected to have at his fingertips information about conditions he is likely to encounter only occasionally or of the services that will be required over the years. For this reason the health visitor or social worker with special experience must work closely with the general practitioner.

6 The Area Specialist in Community Medicine (Child Health) in collaboration with the District Community Physician must initiate in each district discussions (perhaps to be chaired by the paediatrician) between the persons concerned in treating the child and in supporting the parents so that a clear though flexible procedure is agreed, committed to paper and put into effect. Staff from maternity units should be involved in these discussions to ensure that this service is provided routinely following an abnormal delivery.

LIST OF PARTICIPANTS

†SUZAN BENDIX, BA
Senior Social Worker, Cardiff Royal Infirmary

EVANGELINE BOWEN, SRN, SCM
Nursing Officer, Obstetrics Department, University College Hospital

†JANET CARR, PhD
Senior Psychologist, Hilda Lewis House, Bethlem Royal Hospital

JEAN DAVIS, BA, AIMSW
Senior Social Worker, Hospital for Sick Children, Gt. Ormond Street

†MERVYN FOX, MB, BS, DCH
Principal Physician (Child Health) Camden and Islington AHA(T)

*ELIZABETH HARPER, MB, ChB, MFCM, DPH
Area Specialist in Community Medicine (Child Health) Ealing, Hammersmith and Hounslow AHA(T)

*SHEILA HEWETT, PhD
MRC Social Psychiatry Unit, Institute of Psychiatry

*ROBERT LINDON, FFCM, DCH, DPH
Area Medical Officer, Ealing, Hammersmith and Hounslow AHA(T)

*RONALD MACKEITH, DM, FRCP
Lately Consultant Paediatrician, Guy's Hospital

DAVID MORRIS, FRCP, MRCS, DCH
Consultant Paediatrician, Woolwich Group of Hospitals

*MARGARET POLLAK, MD, BS, DOBST RCOG
General Practitioner and Senior Lecturer in Family Child Health, King's College Hospital

*HILDA RAWLINGS, MA, AMISW
Principal Social Worker, King's College Hospital

*BERNIE SPAIN, MA, DIP PSYCH
Research Psychologist, Inner London Education Authority

MARTIN STONE, MRCOG
Obstetric Registrar, Charing Cross Hospital

*GUY WIGLEY, FFCM, DPH
Medical Adviser, Greater London Council and Inner London Education Authority

*ROBERT WIGGLESWORTH, FRCP, DCH
Consultant Paediatrician, Kettering General Hospital and Northamptonshire Hospitals, Oxford Regional Health Authority

†BETTY WILSON, SRN, HVCERT
Specialist Health Visitor, Department of Paediatrics and Child Health, University of Leeds

*LORNA WING, MD, MRCPSYCH
Member of Scientific Staff, MRC Social Psychiatry Unit, Institute of Psychiatry

* Papers in full Report.
† Papers in Appendix.

APPENDIX I
(*two papers*)

HAVING A CONGENITALLY DEFORMED BABY*

My husband and I were together when James was born which really made a lot of difference to both of us. He was 'ours' from the beginning. Neither of us had to be told that we had a deformed baby and neither of us had the task of telling the other.

I'd had a very quick labour without any drugs, gas and air, &c., so was completely conscious and aware of everything. The midwife was holding his screaming head up so that I could see him as he was being born and I saw his arms even before she did. I remember saying 'look his arms aren't right'. The midwife said she wouldn't have let me see him if she'd known but I'm glad she didn't have that choice. As he was lifted up it was as if a photograph was taken in my mind – in one moment I saw his deformed arms and feet. I can still see that picture now. I felt very calm and detached as thought I was watching a film and was not involved at all. Everyone was very upset. People appeared from everywhere.

My husband was there beside me but our contact wasn't close – he was just part of the scene. James was wrapped up and given to me to hold for a moment. I looked at him and just felt nothing at all. I just lay there hearing and seeing everything terribly clearly but not seeming involved. Everyone was talking as though I were in another room.

A doctor silently sewed me up taking about threequarters of an hour to do so and then shook hands with me which I remember thinking extremely funny. At about 11.00 p.m. I was given an injection and a sleeping pill and wheeled back to the ward I'd left just five hours before. The girl who'd been there when I left had gone. I remember wondering whether she'd gone to the labour ward or whether they'd moved her so that I'd be alone and she wouldn't be worried about her baby.

I could hear James screaming in the nursery. When he stopped for a few moments I thought 'perhaps he's died and they won't come and tell

* Talk given at Queen Mary's Hospital, Roehampton, London SW15, during a study day for social workers on maternity units, and published in *The Lancet*, 1973, Vol. 1, p. 1499.

me until the morning because they think I'm asleep'. I kept feeling my tummy to make sure my bump had gone – I couldn't really believe it had all happened in such a few hours. I didn't sleep at all. I just lay looking at the ceiling and listening. I didn't cry – I didn't feel it had all happened to me.

My husband had been given a sleeping-pill to take when he got home. He didn't even remember driving home. All our relatives live 120 miles from us. He 'phoned his mother that evening and left it until the next morning before contacting my parents through my sister. He told a neighbour about James and left it to her to tell our other neighbours. That was a very bad night for him – he felt terribly cut off and alone. Even though I was alone there were people around and about but he was entirely alone.

Straight information

The morning after James's birth I was moved to a separate room so I would not be with other mothers and their babies. I was asked if I wanted my baby with me and I said 'yes'. As soon as I was left alone with him, I unwrapped him and had a good look at him. He seemed to be looking at me but he didn't cry. His left arm was elbow length and his right hand had an obvious elbow-joint and was quite a lot longer. I knew then that he would live, he seemed so strong. It seemed impossible then that he would ever be able to do anything by himself without any artificial aids. It never occurred to me how much his arms would grow in relation to his body (and nobody pointed this out to us!). His hips and legs seemed O.K. to me. He only had four toes on each foot and his feet were very twisted. My husband came in and I asked him if he'd like to have a closer look at him but he said 'no, not yet'. We sat not talking much. James was taken away then to be examined and about half an hour later the paediatrician arrived with a list of James's defects and several suspected ones and said he'd give it to us straight. Besides his feet and arms he had a gap in his lower gum and possible part of the jaw-bone missing. He had a deformed tongue which was about half the size of my little finger-nail. He had small eyes. He was very hairy, probly chromosomes wrong, possibly mongol. He also told us that if he was mentally subnormal very little would be accomplished by giving him artificial arms &c., but if he was mentally normal there would be some future. When the paediatrician left we sat in almost complete silence.

On the ward I found I was open to interference by domestics in hospital, which I didn't like to report. I had to ask another mother in the next room to watch over James if I went to the toilet or I'd return to find cleaners or orderlies unwrapping his clothes to look at him.

Over the next few days specialists came to look at James. Few of them wanted to talk to me but I tried to be around so I could ask what they'd found out. By the end of the week we knew that his mouth deformity in no way hampered feeding and would mean possibly that he'd have a couple of teeth fewer than most people. His chromosome pattern was normal. His feet could be worked on by massage and possibly surgery later on. I insisted on having all these tests done before we went home. On my last day of my ten days we went by ambulance to have James's eyes examined and they were pronounced structurally normal. I was determined to take him home with me. I felt if I left him behind I'd never pluck up courage to fetch him.

The morning after James was born the consultant gynaecologist came in with a group of doctors and remarked, in a very detached manner, that I'd had a perfectly normal birth and such things do happen occasionally and I must have taken some pills early in pregnancy. As he left I cried for the first time at the absolute injustice of life, as I'd not even taken an aspirin during pregnancy. I had thought about having an abnormal child while I was pregnant. I suppose most mothers do. I'd talked about it to quite a few people. I suppose in some ways thinking about it beforehand can lessen the shock. During my teacher-training I visisted a lot of special schools where I saw children with congenital and other deformities and handicaps which had made an impression on me.

Social work support

During my ten days in hospital the social worker came to see me most days and she was the only person who asked how I felt about things. Apart from her short visits and the nurses popping in with pills and feeds I was left alone with the baby a great deal. I must say I did at one time look out at the concrete two floors below my window and consider throwing him out and I felt I could reasonably get away with it and solve all my problems. I was grateful for the relevant books which the social worker brought me as they did give me something to do. She was, I found out later, discouraged from doing much after the first few days because the paediatrician felt she was interfering. She was new in her position in a new hospital and things would have been different now, I'm glad to say. I would have liked to see the social worker again when I came home – I felt cut off. The health visitor didn't fill her place and my GP called once only. I needed someone outside of the situation to talk to – nobody seemed the right person.

I had lots of letters and flowers sent, especially as most of our friends lived so far away. I had nearly 30 bunches of flowers and felt as if I was in a funeral parlour. People didn't like to send things for the baby. I think they did not know whether he would survive. Some of our letters were terrible but I read them all and we burnt them when we got home. Someone did send a rattle. I could tell what it was before I opened the parcel and I cried my eyes out because I knew James wouldn't be able to hold it. I had a lot of visitors, which seemed rather an ordeal at the time, but those people were easier to face when I did go home.

My mother came to stay for a while when I went home. I was in a pretty wobbly state physically. I had been resting with high blood-pressure before I had James and it was easily six months before I started to feel well. I cried a lot by myself, especially when people were trying to be kind. It was easier to keep calm if people were not too sympathetic. Every child my husband or I looked at seemed to be doing things with their hands. My husband teaches and he says he couldn't stop looking at hands and children playing football at his school. My husband had nightmares for some time after James's birth. He was not interested in normal sexual relations for some time.

One day at a time

Although we felt quite differently from each other on several things we could talk about them together. My husband worried a lot about the future but I shut that out of my mind and lived one day at a time. My husband soon felt quite comfortable with James once he was home. James was very responsive right from the beginning. He was physically very strong and active. Dad changed nappies and fed him as often as he could. We took James out as much as we could. We visited all our local friends and then when he was six weeks old we took him to our home town. My youngest sister was getting married and we decided to have him christened the same weekend and introduce him to all our relations. It was a very traumatic weekend but we came home very pleased with ourselves that we'd coped. We were very relieved that it was all over with and we could relax in our home again. James was normal to us. It was only outside that his abnormalities were forced to our attention. Gradually over those first few months we took him to visit all our friends near and far and I felt safer when everyone we knew had seen him. First meetings were hard. People had to take their cue from our attitude and we felt we had to be down to earth and appear to be coping well with everything. I wish during those early months we could have visited Roehampton and seen other children with similar handicaps coping happily and spoken to other parents and staff.

Our paediatrician during these months was most unhelpful. He was much in favour of us sending James into a residential home – his suggestion to me was to have another baby quickly and forget about James. I used to feel terrible after appointments with him because he was so insistent that the best thing for the child was to grow up with specialist help all around him. However from the time James was 14 months his attitude completely changed. By that time James was beginning to talk clearly and could manipulate toys as well as, if not better than, most other children of his age. He had a very good concentration span. We feel we have really educated our paediatrician. He will now do anything to help us. He thinks James is marvellous and says his aims from the beginning were normal environment and education in a normal school, which we chuckle over, thinking of the past. We know our case was probably something new to him. We're only sad to think that had we been different people we might have parted with James thinking it was best for him. All my past training and work as an infant teacher stressed the importance of normal home life and maternal care and we were determined James should have it.

Progress for James

From the time James was born I altered all his clothes rather than try and hide his arms. It took two sad days to cut the sleeves off all his new baby cardigans, &c. – now I'm an expert. I found my training useful in finding suitable toys for the early months. I hooked rattles and mobiles within his reach and by six weeks he was using his longest arm to play with them. He had suction toys with beads and rattles which were very useful for fixing on any shiny surface. His left arm wasn't long enough for him to see, but he started using it around $2\frac{1}{2}$ months when he found he could reach his left ear with it. One evening my husband and I were bathing him together. I placed a duck on his chest and he used both arms to clasp it to him. We both sat on the floor and cried; it was the first time he had held anything independently. From then on he co-ordinated them together to hold things all the time, and within a month he could touch his two arms together. There was no stopping him. At a year he could build six bricks and when he wanted to pick up several bricks he lined them up and picked them up like a builder. He began feeding himself using just his arms at 14 months. First efforts with a biscuit. He was already making efforts with dinners with an adapted spoon on his right arm. He sat alone at six months. Crawling meant that his nose was practically on the floor and he couldn't see where he was going and he's really only perfected it since he could walk!

He just sat playing quite contentedly until 13 months, when he started shuffle-bottoming. He made fantastic speed and last summer his legs and feet became completely hardened to our concrete paths as he preferred them to the grass. He's very cautious by nature, and has never attempted anything until completely sure he could cope. For months he could go up and down stairs, but would only go when I was there. He walked with me holding his longest arm for 4 months before he could walk alone. However, once he started walking alone at 2 years 1 month he was walking backwards, running, trying to jump within a week.

His speech development was good. From 18 months he started making comments about his missing hands. We had a distressing week or two when he was still under 2 years when he woke and cried every morning, saying his hands had dropped off. It seemed to help going through his photos from birth to show him he'd never had hands. He nearly went hysterical one night when I tried to cut his toenails and he thought I was going to cut his toes off. One morning he came into the kitchen and said 'Mummy's got hands'. I said 'yes'. 'Daddy's got hands'. 'Yes'. 'James' got arms'. 'Yes'. 'You won't cut them off?' It's so very difficult to know what to say to such a young child. Our last stay at Roehampton at 2 years 4 months was very useful. He was very aware of the other children, particularly a little girl with arms very similar to his.

When he was 2 years, he was assessed by the local-authority health department and we were told that there was no reason why he shouldn't have normal school education. The doctor was 18 months from retirement and had never met a case like James's or anything similar. He came to our house expecting, as he said, to meet an extremely frustrated child unable to do anything. He stayed two hours enthralled as he watched James drawing, doing jigsaws, and playing with his mouth-organ.

We want James to be able to go to school with children who have got to know him. I take him to play-group functions and he will start going himself in the autumn. I take him to school with me for an afternoon most weeks and he comes in the classroom with me as I go round telling stories to different classes. I'm trying to break the ice with him now so that he won't be such a complete novelty later.

INTERVIEWS WITH PARENTS

Mervyn Fox

Physician

I ask Mrs. K. to tell me of her first learning she had a mongol child.

'I took him to the clinic one day, when he was seven months old, because I thought the look of his mouth was wrong. They looked at his mouth and said nothing, only that I'd have to see a specialist at another clinic. They looked at his eyes, and his fingers, and his toes and I thought, what the hell are they looking at all that for when all I was worried about was the roof of his mouth? I had the youngest girl with me . . . He sat back like this, the specialist, he folded his arms and said "Well Mrs. K., I'm afraid we found plenty wrong with your child". That was a start . . . my stomach went down, you know. He said "I'm afraid he's a mongol. It's no use you sending him to school, he probably won't walk until he's eight, nor talk till he's twelve, if he talks at all". That's just how he said it to me. He rattled on about this, that, and the other but I just sat there . . . his voice just sort of faded out . . . I wasn't listening . . . it wasn't sinking in, what he was saying. I dressed him, and as I was walking out he was still talking. From that day to this I don't even remember coming home. All I can remember was, it was pouring with rain.

We'd been going to a clinic two or three times before they mentioned it, before I asked about the roof of his mouth. The health visitor didn't come until after I'd found out. He was my third child, and we did think he was a bit slow, to sit up, but I didn't dream he was a mongol until they told me'.

Mr. K. breaks in angily. 'the midwife must have known . . . in fact the doctor said she did know. She could have told us, after the fourteen days, about then. She just used to say, "what a lovely little boy" . . . it's hard to see wrong in your own child . . . we had no inkling that he was going to be a mongol. . . .'

Mrs. K.: 'After I came back from the clinic, I couldn't sleep, I couldn't do anything. I went to the doctor, she was angry, she said she could have told me the first time she saw the baby . . . I asked her "Why didn't you then?" but she wouldn't answer. . . . They should have told me earlier, as soon as they were certain'.

Mr. K: 'Our doctor, she should have sat down and discussed it with us'.

Mrs. K: 'I think that doctor could have done it in a nicer way than he did, a sort of stab-in-the-back he gave me'.

Interviewer: Can you remember your wife coming home that afternoon in the rain and telling you about it?

Mr. K: 'Yes. It upset me. Nobody ever really told us, accurately, what to expect. We only leant by living with him, watching him grow up. There's not many people to talk to . . . you might feel a bit ashamed . . . there's a bit of a tendency to hide. My wife is still very sensitive about it. . . .'

Interview with Mrs. Y

Mrs. Y, what about at the beginning, when you first found out she had spina bifida?

'When she was born, it was like a dream. I never knew anything about this, I didn't realise there was so much illness and handicap in the world,

I was a person that was free. It was a shock. I used to feel ever so sorry for myself, crying, she had to go through so much and I couldn't do anything. I couldn't see anyone scold her. I couldn't bear anybody to breathe on her, in case they gave her germs – this was all in my mind – when she first went to school I was like somebody that was lost, I just used to walk around the house on my own. I feel she might have been born all over again, perfect. . . .'

She was told her baby 'had a sac' soon after she was born, at home. 'The nurse said she might not live, and it would be a good thing if she didn't. Then the doctor came back and said she was in hospital, and that I'd see her again in a few months. All my hopes were bucked up. Then I was taken up to see her in the hospital. One little doctor came up and said "her left foot's swollen, but it'll go down – but I don't reckon she'll live to be five" – and then a surgeon came and told him off, said she'd got a great chance in life. I was unbalanced then, I couldn't think straight, I couldn't care less about the home or the other children. When I look back I think everyone was trying not to be hurtful, everything was done for the best. I don't think you should know too much or be asked to make decisions. I couldn't have foretold what she'd turn out to be, but I wouldn't have dared to say not to operate, to leave her. . . .'

And when you brought her home from hospital?

'This was difficult. They told me not to let her catch any colds – so I pushed them all out of the way, I wouldn't let anyone breathe on her. I was frightened to let her have the bottle, or any dirty clothes. They said I was over-possessive. It turned people against me. No health visitor called. I took her to the hospital every week, this was helpful. Later the midwife came to see me, and took Tina up to the clinic, and they sent her on to the school. School is wonderful, I get all the help I need there. She couldn't ever go to an ordinary school; I'd be too frightened, the children would be too rough.'

APPENDIX II—A SERVICE FOR SPINA BIFIDA CHILDREN
(*two papers*)

ADMINISTRATIVE AND SOCIAL MANAGEMENT of the family with a new-born spina bifida infant, within the Cardiff area

Susan Bendix
Medical Social Worker

In 1970 Cardiff Royal Infirmary appointed a 'clerical co-ordinator' for spina bifida cases; her function was to improve co-ordination between hospital departments, and between the hospital and the community services. All records of spina bifida children were removed from the records department and centralised in her office, and all clinic appointments arranged by her, thus co-ordinating the various specialities involved.

In the same year, at the instigation of the head social worker, approaches were made to the chief nursing officers of the seven Glamorgan and one Cardiff health divisions, to see what could be done to improve liaison between hospital and community. A committee was formed, to identify the problems involved, and to develop some kind of formal procedure for the administrative handling of the new-born spina bifida infant and his family. The committee consisted of the chief nursing officer for each local authority health division, or a senior health visitor designated to take a special interest in spina bifida, and representatives from the social services departments. The hospital was represented by a senior consultant paediatrician, senior medical and nursing staff from the spina bifida unit, the clerical co-ordinator, the unit social worker, head social worker, and a hospital administrator. The committee met seven times between April 1970 and July 1971.

Procedure

The procedure which evolved, can be condensed into the following ten points:

1 Each health division has nominated a health visitor or nursing officer who has special responsibility for children in her area with spina bifida. These are known as the designated health visitors, and they receive direct all communications from the hospital concerning spina bifida children.

2 To simplify the communication network the clerical co-ordinator contacts one particular officer in County Hall when she needs to notify the health visitor of a child's birth or discharge. This officer then telephones the designated health visitor concerned, with the message. This saves time and avoids frustration.

3 The usual method of notification of abnormal births is for the maternity hospital staff to inform the Community Physician, who notifies the health visiting department. It may, therefore, take days before a health visitor discovers that a child with spina bifida has been born in her area: the new procedure attempts to short-cut this. Within hours of birth, the baby, often accompanied by the father, is transferred to the spina bifida unit. The clerical co-ordinator then phones her contacts in the health authority which notifies the designated health visitor. A link is thus immediately made between hospital and community.

4 The father is usually fully occupied in these first few days, travelling between maternity hospital, home and spina bifida unit. For the mother, bereft of her baby, these are the worst few days. She may well be in bed brooding about what her child looks like and feeling thoroughly out of touch. To improve this matter the committee suggested that the designated health visitor should visit the mother in the maternity hospital or at her home if she is discharged after 48 hours. Her task is to talk to the mother about spina bifida in general and to brief her about the people she will meet in the unit.

5 The father is interviewed by a member of the medical staff, in the unit, at the baby's admission if he accompanies the child, or if not on his first visit. On the mother's discharge from hospital, both parents are given an appointment with the consultant. They are put as fully in the picture about their child's condition as possible. They are then seen by the unit social worker to see what social or emotional help is needed.

6 As soon as a reasonable assessment of the baby is made, the consultant writes to the family doctor and a copy of this letter also goes to the District Community Physician. He describes the baby's condition, and what the parents have been told, and the prognosis for bowel and bladder function, hydrocephalus and future mobility. He also mentions whether the parents have asked for genetic counselling.

7 A notorious fact of hospital life is that discharge letters often take weeks to reach the family doctor. This means he knows little about the child, should his mother bring him to the surgery after discharge, which does little for the mother's confidence in her family doctor. To avoid this, and to foster contact between community doctors and families instead of increasing dependence on the hospital, the mother is handed a letter on the child's discharge, to take to her family doctor. This letter describes the child's progress, present condition and current treatment. The mother is thus encouraged to consult her own doctor when she gets home and her doctor is in turn encouraged to participate in the child's treatment.

8 On discharge, the clerical co-ordinator rings her County Hall contact, who then notifies the designated health visitor. This enables someone from the community to call as soon as the baby arrives home.

9 The mother is told, on the day of discharge, all details of clinics, and is given the date of the first combined clinic the child is to attend.

10 Each month the clerical co-ordinator compiles a list of children attending the combined clinic, and this is sent to the designated health visitors, with a request for social reports. These reports ask for details on family and background, living conditions, the child's health and personality, and the family's attitude to the child and his handicap. The clerical co-ordinator circulates copies of these to the consultant and social worker, so that when the meeting is held at the end of the combined clinic, to discuss each child, full social, as well as medical, details are available. The procedure also states it as desirable that, for the baby's first combined clinic, the health visitor should accompany the parents.

Secondary function

The committee meetings did not only result in the drawing up of this procedure. It had many other side products.

Firstly, the meeting of hospital and community personnel has led to an increased understanding of each other's functions and difficulties, and to the lowering of barriers. The hospital has lost its image of the impregnable bastille, and now health visitors ring up quite informally to ask questions or discuss cases. For the families, this has been beneficial in that they can see that there is more of a continuum between home and hospital.

Secondly, on consecutive committee meetings a case of a particular spina bifida child was studied, from birth through her first year of life. This enabled us to see how the procedure was working and also to study the effect on a family of having a handicapped child. Discussions ensued on areas of emotional difficulty and how best to deal with them. Differences in the functions of health visitors and social workers were also worked out.

Thirdly, a great deal of anxiety about the nursing and handling of the newborn child was expressed, and an attempt to allay this was made by three methods:

1 a senior doctor circulated descriptions of specialised clinical tests, so that the health visitors would be better equipped to prepare the mothers when their children underwent these procedures.

2 a general invitation was issued to all divisions for health visitors to come to the unit, meet the staff and discuss nursing procedures with the ward sister. Some divisions sent groups, but many people came as individuals.

3 a hospital team, consisting of paediatric consultant, sisters and social worker, visisted each health division for a panel discussion on all aspects of spina bifida. These meetings were well attended by health visitors, and often district nurses, family doctors and medical officers.

Fourthly, a benefit from the committee meetings was the clarifying of the material needs of spina bifida children. Pressure was put on the local authority health departments to meet some of these requirements. In Glamorgan, for instance, it became general policy that incontinence pads and nappy liners could be supplied free to spina bifida children.

Fifthly, the committee did not restrict itself to the topic of the newborn child. Discussions ranged over the various ages and stages, and what provisions, educational, medical and social, were necessary for each stage up to the employment problem. There was a sharing of anxiety and a sharing of information.

Future plans

It is only too easy for an organisation to outlive its original function, and to exist purely in order to perpetuate itself. Thus, when it was felt that a good procedure had been set up, and efficient lines of communication established, the committee disbanded until further notice. The health visitors were asked, by post, if they would like to meet again in the future. With one exception, they felt it would be useful to revise the procedure. Most were adamant that they did not want to get bogged down by bureaucratic details, and the chief desire was to meet to hear about the latest medical and nursing developments in spina bifida. In November 1972, a single similar meeting was held, to work out a procedure with the four Monmouthshire area health divisions, and a modified procedure was worked out, with no immediate plans to meet again.

Effectiveness

In 1973 an informal questionnaire was sent to the health visitors, to see how, and if, the procedure was working. It was rewarding to find out how faithfully it had been adhered to, and how unanimous was the opinion that the procedure had done much to improve liaison between hospital and community. This procedure could well be adapted to include all handicapped newborn babies, especially in view of the increasing stress on departments of developmental medicine. The specialist health visitor can listen to the parents' fears and help them to come to terms with any arrangements that may have been made. Parents whose children have apparently slight handicaps are often the most concerned and need the most help with this important and difficult decision. The link between home, school and hospital that the specialist health visitor can provide is beneficial to all concerned.

THE SPECIALIST HEALTH VISITOR

Betty Wilson
Health Visitor

The functions of a health visitor are to listen, to inform and to advise. We can all be good listeners, but our ability to inform and advise depend upon our training and experience. About 2 per 1000 children are born with spina bifida, and about 1 child per 1000 will reach school age. With approximately 8000 health visitors working in the field, each health visitor is likely to have only two or three spina bifida children in her area.

A recent booklet on 'The Care of the Child with Spina Bifida,' published by the DHSS underlies the diverse kinds of help and advice needed by these children and their families. These include surgical management of the back, of hydrocephalus, of orthopaedic problems and of the urinary tract; the management of the incontinent, paraplegic child often with urinary diversion and ventricular shunt; the provision of calipers and wheelchairs; physiotherapy; helping parents during times of emotional crisis; genetic counselling; social services and educational placement.

With such a wide area of knowledge required, it is hardly surprising that the booklet quotes studies which 'showed that although parents were helped to some extent by both health visitors and family doctors they were often dissatisfied and frequently felt better informed about spina bifida than either'. One of the conclusions of the report is the need for specialist health visitors.

A specialist health visitor's work will take her into all the institutions offering care for the handicapped, and she will be able to provide a link between hospital, home and school and communicate with other caring services.

The specialist health visitor in hospital

The supportive role of the specialist health visitor starts in hospital, if possible in the maternity hospital. Some mothers have felt that it would be useful to be able to talk or to be given written information about their baby at this time and certainly the idea must be suggested that they are involved in the care of their child from the very beginning.

At this important and potentially traumatic time in the family's life, it is essential that no extra anxiety is caused, and with her extra knowledge, the specialist health visitor can give advice fully and without embarrassment. Advice has probably been given in hospital, but the specialist health visitor will be able to see how much has been absorbed, and resolve any doubts in the more relaxed atmosphere of home. Parents are very appreciative of this link with hospital, where they have received their first support, and are pleased to be told what to expect at the first outpatients visit. Even when prepared, some parents still find hospital outpatient visits emotionally exhausting and obtain little satisfaction from them.

Ideally, the specialist health visitor should be able to make a home visit before hospital appointments so that she is aware of any areas of concern the parents may have about the child, and see that parents are given the opportunity to talk about these problems, even if they seem trivial in a clinic situation.

By observing parents and children at the clinic, the health visitor will be aware of any necessary follow-up visits she needs to make, and can deal with any referrals from the medical staff.

A specialist health visitor's knowledge of the home situation and family relationships can prove invaluable to the medical staff in the care of their child. Nursing staff certainly appreciate that they have passed on information to an interested person, rather than leaving messages with someone they do not know.

The specialist health visitor in the home

Invariably, parents find it easier to discuss their problems in their own home setting, and an interested and impartial listener who is part of the team caring for their child, is in an ideal position to help them cope with their emotions and guilt feelings, and help them with their practical problems.

Because their child is different from those of most of their friends and neighbours many parents feel lonely and lost and to have a special person visiting to whom they can turn for support boosts a very lowered morale. Parents want to talk about what they can expect their child's progress to be and need to be given as much knowledge as possible to help them overcome any fears they may have.

Some parents need help to encourage their children to do things for themselves, and some parents are discouraged by a child's slow progress. Often parents are the first to realise that their child could do more, and become depressed from the frustration of not being able to obtain the help the child requires. Most parents can cope with the handicap itself but when the child is ill with urinary or chest infections, or when the valve is not working properly, the mother particularly needs support in her care of the child at this time.

The specialist health visitor will become aware of the times when mothers are likely to be more anxious about their child, and when relationships within the family are likely to be most strained, e.g. when the child should be walking, approaching the start of school or if the mother is having another baby.

Inevitably, some of the children with spina bifida will die, and the parents will need support in their bereavement and possibly for some time after. To be able to talk to someone who is not involved emotionally but who shows she cares and has known the child, is often beneficial.

The specialist health visitor and school

Parents of a handicapped child are concerned from a very early age about school for their child. More and more parents are realizing the benefits of playgroups and nursery schools for the handicapped child, and have seen from the experience of others how extra stimulation at this age can make their child more independent and sociable, and better able to settle in school. Parents need time to come to terms with the fact that their children may need special school, and after spending so much time caring for their child are sometimes unconsciously reluctant to allow others to take charge.

The specialist health visitor can listen to the parents' fears and help them to come to terms with any arrangements that may have been made. Parents whose children have apparently slight handicaps are often the most concerned and need the most help with this important and difficult decision. The link between home, school and hospital that the specialist health visitor can provide is beneficial to all concerned.

The specialist health visitor as an educator

Whilst much is being written about spina bifida at present, because this is a minority group, the special problems are not generally known and the specialist health visitor can help in the education of both parents, her colleagues and other professional groups interested in the care of these children.

By her close contact with hospital, school and the voluntary organisations concerned, she will be able to keep her own knowledge up-to-date, which will in turn increase her contribution to the care of the child and help her obtain more satisfaction from her work.

Hilda Lewis House is an experimental unit, generously staffed with well qualified people, and is thus especially well placed to carry out the kind of work that many people would wish to do had they the facilities.

APPENDIX III

BEHAVIOUR MODIFICATION
as applied to the severely retarded child at Hilda Lewis House

Janet Carr
Clinical Psychologist

Hilda Lewis House is a small unit for mentally handicapped children, which forms part of the community service providing for the psychiatric treatment needs for the Camberwell district in South-East London, serving a population of about 175,000. A few children are also admitted for assessment and short-term treatment from outside this area.

The Unit has 24 beds and caters for children between the ages of 0–16 who are severely retarded with additional handicaps; these may be sensory or physical handicaps – blindness, deafness, epilepsy, cerebral palsy, and so on – or the handicap may consist of a severe behaviour problem.

Children are normally seen first at an out-patient clinic or through a domiciliary visit, and this is followed by any of a variety of possible patterns of contact between the child and the Unit. The child may be admitted to the Unit for a period of assessment and treatment, which may last for only a few weeks or up to several years depending on the needs of the child and of his family (the average length of stay is 3–4 months).

After discharge from the Unit most children are followed-up at home and at school, and a child may be readmitted for further treatment if necessary or in times of family crisis. Alternatively, the child may attend the Unit daily, either after he has been discharged as an in-patient or as a bridging measure between the Unit and home, or as an alternative to admission. Some children are seen and treated entirely on an out-patient basis, being seen at home or at school or both.

Assessment

When a child is admitted to the Unit he is thoroughly assessed by a multi-disciplinary team, consisting of doctors, psychologists, occupational therapists, teachers, social worker and nurses, with other specialists such as physiotherapists and speech therapists available to give advice where needed. Physical problems, such as difficulties with hearing, vision or mobility, the child's need of drugs to control or alleviate fits or other conditions, are carefully investigated. If necessary the child visits other centres such as the Newcomen at Guy's Hospital, or Queen Mary's, Carshalton, for more detailed assessment, particularly of perceptual handicaps. The results of treatment begun or continued are monitored during the child's stay in the Unit and any necessary adjustments are made.

Treatment

To attempt to deal with a child's learning and behaviour problems a treatment programme for him is drawn up at a meeting convened by the psychologist responsible for him and attended by members of all other disciplines.

The first task is to outline the problems the child presents, both those reported to us by his parents, teachers, social workers and so on, and those that we have encountered during the 10 days or so since his admission. In many cases the two sets of problems overlap but a child may show problems in the Unit that do not occur at home and vice versa.

Next we go on to identify the reinforcement, or reward, available to the child. Reinforcement is defined as anything which, when it follows closely on a behaviour, makes it more likely that the behaviour will occur again. In other words if you tell a child to shut the door, and if when he does you immediately give him something he likes very much, he is more likely to shut the door promptly the next time you tell him to.

Reinforcement is fundamental to behaviour modification, and no treatment programme can work unless a really effective reinforcer is available for the individual child. Sometimes this is no problem, as when the child enjoys food – any food, bits of apple, crisps, chocolate, cheese, drinks – or when the child responds well to praise. If he is not interested in these we have to look for something else. Some children like caresses – stroking, cuddling, kissing, blowing softly; some respond to clapping, others to music, while one little boy liked to have an electric toothbrush in his mouth. Whatever it is, until we find the particular reinforcer for the child one treatment programme has little chance of success.

Personal programme

Having outlined the child's problems and the reinforcers available for him, we go on to the possible ways of dealing with each problem, ways arrived at after full discussion between the members of the team and derived from what they think are the most useful ideas put forward. Copies of the programme are distributed to everyone concerned with the child, one copy is hung up in a central place and everyone is expected to read it – in this way we hope that the child will be treated consistently by everyone who has contact with him.

The programme can at any time be altered or added to, if for instance the child makes progress and the problems alter, or if the programme does not work. Parents may come to the Unit to participate in the child's treatment (there are two 'Parents' rooms' for those who wish to stay on the Unit) when we can discuss the treatment programme with them, and they can make suggestions for it and may want to follow the programmes themselves when the child returns home for the week-end (as virtually all children do).

Treatment programmes may be discussed with the child's teachers when they attend the case conference (as do also his local authority social worker, doctor, or others who have a particular concern for him). When the child is discharged from the Unit a copy of the treatment programme is sent to his teachers, or psychologists visit the school to see how they can help the school in the handling of the child.

Home care

When the child is not admitted but is seen at home he is visisted by a member of staff, or by two or more as necessary, depending on his problem. Staff members discuss with the parents what their problems are and help them to devise a programme by which they themselves (and brothers and sisters sometimes) can help the child. Often this programme will have several stages.

The parents may not be clear about what the problem is; they may know in a general way that the child is difficult, for example, but may be so closely observant of the situation to be able to say exactly what brings this about, exactly what the child does, and what they do in response. We may therefore ask the parents to keep precise records of problem situations as they arise so that the best way to deal with them will become clearer. Once the problem has been defined we help the parents to draw up a programme to deal with it. (Of course sometimes it is not 'a' problem but several problems, in which case we may have to decide, with the parents, which are the most important ones to be tackled first.)

Next we teach the parents the behaviour modification techniques they will need to use, coupled perhaps with some of the principles underlying the techniques. Usually the most important single technique we teach them is that of reinforcement; if they want their child to learn something – to sit quietly for a moment, point to pictures in a book, put on his socks, use his potty instead of his pants – he is more likely to learn it if he is reinforced *immediately* and *consistently* every time he does the desired thing. Once again we may have to search for powerful reinforcers but in many cases a hug or kiss from his parents, provided it is sufficiently warmly and quickly given, is reinforcer enough, shown by the fact that he begins to learn what they are trying to teach him.

In this way parents come to realise the great importance to their child of the attention they pay to him as a reinforcer for his behaviour. This is valuable when it is being used to build up good behaviour, but all too often the child has learned that he can get the attention he craves by behaving badly. When he behaves badly he can be sure that his parents will notice, scold or smack him perhaps but at least will be attending to him; if he sat quitely playing with his toys he might not be noticed all afternoon. So parents may have to learn how to ignore an infuriating child, and, almost equally difficult, how to turn the spotlight of attention on a child who is doing nothing but not be a trouble.

Another technique we often have to teach is that of *prompting* – putting a child physically through an action that he does not yet know how to do, such as carrying a spoonful of food to his mouth; the parent's hand, over the child's hand, picks up the spoon with the bite of food in it and guides it to the child's mouth (when the food itself is a suitable reinforcer). Gradually, as the parent can feel the child learning and taking over the movement he *fades* the prompt, very gradually releasing his hold where it is not needed.

Another technique is the *breaking down into small steps* of an activity, so that instead of having to learn a whole task, which may be more than he could manage, we teach him only a small part of it at a time, starting at the end of the completed action; for example, if we want to teach him to put on his vest, we first put it on over his head and arms and only ask him to put it down; when he can do this successfully we put it on over his arms and teach him, by prompting if necessary, to pull it over his head and down, and so on.

Dealing with unacceptable behaviour

The question of punishment for bad behaviour often arises, and punishment may have to be used, though we stress that it is likely to be of little use unless the child can learn at the same time how he can get reinforcement for his good behaviour. The commonest form of punishment we use is *time-out from positive reinforcement*: that is to say, a child who receives reinforcement when he is behaving well finds it withdrawn if he misbehaves.

If the parents' attention is reinforcing to the child it may be withdrawn like this: a parent who has been watching and commenting on what the child is doing, for instance a puzzle, when he does something naughty like throwing the pieces will look away from him. This is easier said than done.

In practice it may be extremely difficult, especially with a disruptive child, and parents may need more than one session with the staff member (who does not find it easy either but has had more practice and more experience of the effectiveness of the technique than have had the parents) who will demonstrate how it should be done and help the parents improve their own performance. If a child is so disruptive that the parents cannot safely ignore him then a "time-out" room may be used; it may be difficult in some households to find a suitable room but parents have successfully used bathrooms, cloakrooms, and the child's own bedroom as a time-out room, where he may be put for short periods (about five minutes) following on his bad behaviour. Again we stress that, like positive reinforcement, punishment, to be effective, must follow immediately and consistently on every instance of the behaviour it is designed to lessen, and be used for that only.

Continuing surveillance

Once the programme has been decided on we arrange further visits to the family, when we check the records and review progress and help to work out any adjustments to the programme that may be necessary. If the programme has been working well this is usually simple, as the parents will have had personal experience of the effectiveness of the techniques and are likely to want to pursue them further.

If on the other hand the programme has not been working and the parents can see no improvement in the child, we may have to reassess the situation to see where we went wrong and replan the programme.

In either case it is important that the visits should be maintained, although they may be spaced at increasingly longer intervals; even where parents are highly successful in their treatment they enjoy and benefit from the staff member's interest, support and help, though parents may themselves become very skilled in applying the principles they have learned to new problems as they arise.

Ancillary problems

The problems that we tackle in this way are of course usually those of the management of problems and the teaching of new skills by the parents in relation to their retarded child. Help has also been given on occasions with other sorts of problems, for instance, getting a child to school who was difficult and resistant on the journey; setting up a joint interview between the school, the mother, and a staff member where the mother was nervous of approaching the school on her own; providing transport to make sure that parents can get to the local Toy Library (run by the senior occupational therapist at Hilda Lewis House) and to parents' evenings at the Unit. In a few cases where the behaviour of a normal child in the family has been causing difficulty we have helped the parents to deal with this.